The Fantastic Baseball Quiz Book

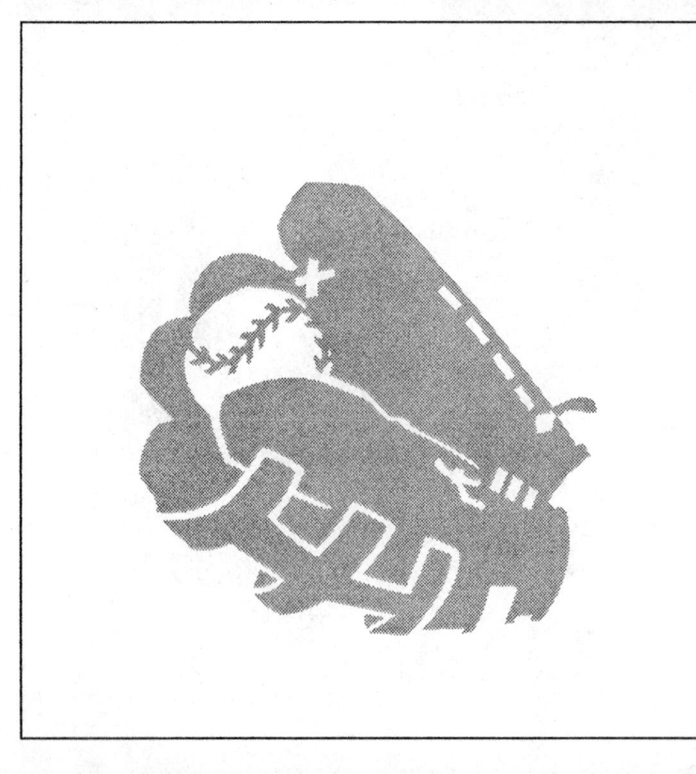

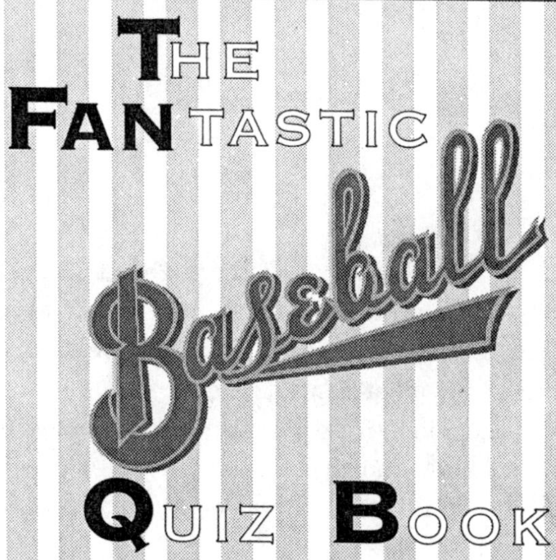

The Fantastic Baseball Quiz Book

Justin Martin

Ariel Books

Andrews and McMeel
Kansas City

 For information write Andrews and McMeel, a Universal Press Syndicate Company, 4520 Main Street, Kansas City, Missouri 64111.

ISBN: 0-8362-1511-7

Library of Congress Catalog Card Number: 96-83550

CONTENTS

Introduction 7

Teams 9

Players 51

Playoffs and World Series 92

Immortals 134

Lore and Lingo 175

Record Book 216

Rule Book 257

Bloopers, Bad Hops, and General Buffoonery 296

Bottom of the Ninth 338

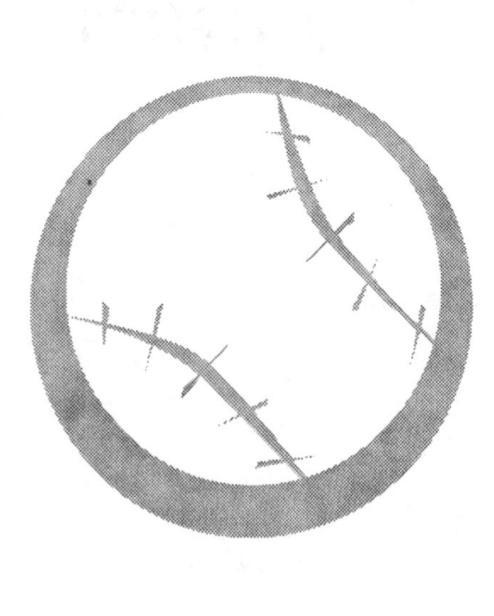

INTRODUCTION

Faster than a Nolan Ryan heater, able to clear tall fences with a single swing . . . look . . . there in your hands . . . it's a soggy nacho, it's a spitball. No, it's *The Fantastic Baseball Quiz Book.* Peruse these pages and prepare to be dazzled by the rich history of America's favorite pastime.

This book covers all the bases: It's packed with trivia about the game's immortals and its clowns, memorable feats, World Series history, rules, and freak occurrences aplenty. Along with multiple choice questions, there are Q&As, true/false, matching, and fill-in-the-blanks—nearly four hundred questions in all. We've varied the level of difficulty, providing everything from basic questions for rookies to questions contained in a bonus chapter entitled "Bottom of the Ninth," which are so difficult you may want to wear a batting helmet.

Play Ball!

TEAMS

TRUE OR FALSE:

The 1906 Cubs went 116–36, the best record in baseball history.

Answer: True

MATCH TEAMS WITH THEIR OLD NAMES:

1. Astros	A. Redlegs
2. Yankees	B. Pilgrims
3. Red Sox	C. Highlanders
4. Reds	D. Colt .45s

Answers: 1-D, 2-C, 3-B, 4-A

Extra Bases> Before Houston's team was the Astros, they were the Colt .45s (1962–64); Highlanders was the Yankees' original name, 1903–12; Boston's team was known as the Somersets (1901–02), then the Pilgrims (1903–06), and as the Red Sox ever since; Cincinnati's team was born as the Red Stockings in 1876 and the name was shortened to Reds two years later. But at the height of the Cold War, when it was "better dead than red," the team officially changed its name to the Redlegs, 1953–58.

Q: What team lost a record 21 games in a row to start the 1988 season?

A: Orioles

Why is Cleveland's ball club named the Indians?

A. The city has a rich history with regard to Native Americans. Cleveland is actually a name used by the tribe that first settled in the area and means "beautiful city on the lake."

B. No special reason. Indians sounds cool. What about the Braves?

C. At the turn of the century, when the Indians entered the league, Cleveland was considered part of the West.

D. The team is named after a popular player who was a Native American.

E. Hey, what more can one expect from a city that once had a river catch on fire from all the pollutants in the water?

Answer: D

Extra Bases> Louis Sockalexis, a Penobscot Indian, was a star right fielder for the Cleveland Naps, 1897–99. A contest was held in 1915 to rename the Naps, and they were christened the Indians in Sockalexis's honor.

HANK AARON STARTED AND ENDED HIS CAREER IN THE SAME CITY, ______.

Answer: Milwaukee

Extra Bases>

Aaron began his career in 1954, with the Milwaukee Braves, who moved to Atlanta after the 1965 season. Aaron went back to Milwaukee and played for the Brewers in his last two seasons, 1975–76.

True or False:

Toronto is not the first big–league club to use the name Blue Jays.

Answer: True

Extra Bases>

The Phillies officially changed their name to Blue Jays, 1944–45.

Q: What were baseball's initial two expansion teams in 1960?

A: Los Angeles Angels, Washington Senators

Extra Bases> The Angels later moved to Anaheim and became the California Angels. The Senators were a replacement for a long-standing team of the same name, which had just fled the Capitol city for Minneapolis and become the Twins. The new Senators were also destined to depart—to Arlington, Texas, where they became the Rangers.

MATCH TEAMS AND DIVISIONS:

1. Mariners
2. Braves
3. Cardinals
4. Brewers

A. National League Central
B. American League Central
C. National League East
D. American League West

Answers: 1-D, 2-C, 3-A, 4-B

THOUGH LOCATED IN THE LANDLOCKED CITY OF ______, THE ______ GAINED THEIR NAME AS A RESULT OF RAIDING OTHER TEAMS FOR TALENT IN BASEBALL'S EARLY DAYS.

Answer: Pittsburgh, Pirates

ALL BUT ONE OF THE FOLLOWING EITHER IS OR HAS BEEN A NEW YORK CITY TEAM:

A. Yankees
B. Dodgers
C. Giants
D. Braves
E. Mets

Answer: D

TRUE OR FALSE:

The 1984 Tigers held on to first place in their division, every day from Opening Day forward.

Answer: True

Extra Bases> Detroit ran away with the AL East, posting a 104–58 record. Only three other teams have led for the entire season: the 1923 Giants, 1927 Yankees, and 1955 Dodgers.

Q: What was the nickname for the great Cincinnati teams of the '70s?

A: The Big Red Machine

MATCH TEAMS WITH BANNER YEARS:

1. Indians	A. 1985
2. Royals	B. 1993
3. Mets	C. 1954
4. Braves	D. 1969

Answers: 1-C, 2-A, 3-D, 4-B

Extra Bases> The 1954 Indians had a phenomenal 111–43 record, but choked in the Series, losing to the Giants in four. The Amazin' Mets shocked everyone in 1969, by going 100–62 and beating Baltimore in five for the World Championship. In 1985 the Royals went 91–71, then bested their cross-state rivals, the Cardinals, in seven, for their first World Series win. The 1993 Braves were 104–58, but lost the playoffs, four games to two, to a scrappy Phillies team.

AMONG AMERICAN LEAGUE CITIES, ______ IS THE FARTHEST NORTH.

Answer: Seattle

Extra Bases>

Yes, indeed, Toronto lies south of Seattle.

TRUE OR FALSE:

The Padres have never won a World Series.

Answer: True

Extra Bases>

Their only visit was in 1984, when they lost to the Tigers, four games to one.

What were the Brooklyn Bridegrooms, Rochester Hop-Bitters, and Toledo Maumees?

A. Negro League teams
B. Union Association teams
C. American Association teams
D. defunct American League teams
E. imaginary Strat-O-Matic teams

Answer: C

MATCH TEAMS AND STADIUMS:

1. Royals	A. Fenway Park
2. Rockies	B. Three Rivers Stadium
3. Red Sox	C. Kauffman Stadium
4. Pirates	D. Coors Field

Answers: 1-C, 2-D, 3-A, 4-B

THE "A'S" IN OAKLAND A'S STANDS FOR ______.

Answer: Athletics

Q: What was the first team—in any sport—to play in a domed stadium?

A: Houston Astros

All but one of the following applies to one of baseball's worst teams ever, the 1962 Mets:

A. They had a 40–120 record.
B. They ended their season by hitting into a triple play.
C. Manager Casey Stengel told his outfielders: "When one of them guys hits a single to you, throw the ball to third. That way we can hold them to a double."
D. They started Pete Walthrop, the only underhanded pitcher of the twentieth century, clocked at a mere 48 mph.
E. Outfielder "Marvelous" Marv Throneberry hit a triple, but was called out when it was discovered that he failed to touch first or second.

Answer: D

On September 11, 1991, _____ pitchers Kent Mercker, Mark Wohlers, and Alejando Pena tossed the first combined no-hitter in NL history, a 1–0 gem against the Padres.

Answer: Atlanta Braves

Q: What team plays in an old-fashioned stadium that didn't even add lights until 1988?

A: Chicago Cubs (Wrigley Field)

ALONG WITH EARNING A BUNDLE, THE OWNERS OF BASEBALL TEAMS TEND TO EARN THE ENMITY OF PLAYERS, MANAGERS, THE PRESS, AND PUBLIC. MATCH TEAMS WITH DESPISED OWNERS, PAST AND PRESENT:

1. A's	A. George Steinbrenner
2. Brewers	B. Marge Schott
3. Reds	C. Charles O. Finley
4. Yankees	D. Bud Selig

Answers: 1-C, 2-D, 3-B, 4-A

TRUE OR FALSE:

The Expos and Blue Jays faced off in 1992, for the only all-Canada World Series.

Answer: False

THE OAKLAND A'S HAVE A STRANGE, AND OFTEN, UH, COLORFUL HISTORY. ALL BUT ONE OF THE FOLLOWING IS AN A'S ODDITY:

A. using gold-colored bases in their 1970 home opener, an idea quickly nixed by baseball's Rules Committee
B. experimenting with orange baseballs in a 1973 exhibition game
C. the owner once trying to convince ace Vida Blue to change his first name to "True"
D. playing a July 4, 1976, doubleheader in red-white-and-blue uniforms
E. having a pitcher named Blue Moon Odom

Answer: D

THE FARM CLUBS OF MAJOR LEAGUE TEAMS ARE DESIGNATED SINGLE-, DOUBLE-, AND TRIPLE- ________.

Answer: A

MATCH CITIES WITH TEAMS THAT DIED OR MOVED AWAY:

1. Philadelphia
2. St. Louis
3. Seattle
4. Hartford

A. Pilots
B. Browns
C. Dark Blues
D. A's

Answers: 1-D, 2-B, 3-A, 4-C

Extra Bases> The A's fled Philly after the 1954 season. The Pilots, who played in an open-air stadium, braved Seattle's weather for just one season—1969—before moving to Milwaukee and becoming the Brewers. The St. Louis Browns moved to Baltimore and became the Orioles after the 1953 season; the Hartford Dark Blues were a charter NL team that folded after the league's second year of existence, 1877.

Q: What two expansion teams joined the National League for the 1993 season?

A: Colorado Rockies, Florida Marlins

True or False:

The 1876 New York Mutuals were baseball's first professional team.

Answer: False

Extra Bases>

It was the 1869 Cincinnati Red Stockings. The team went 60–0 for the season.

For the 1990 season, the _____ added free-agent Mark Davis, the '89 NL Cy Young Award winner, to a staff that already included Bret Saberhagen, the '85 and '89 AL Cy Young winner.

Answer: Kansas City Royals

MATCH TEAMS AND FORMER STADIUMS:

1. Dodgers
2. A's
3. Reds
4. Expos

A. Shibe Park
B. Jarry Park
C. Ebbets Field
D. Crosley Field

Answers: 1-C, 2-A, 3-D, 4-B

Q: What team made Sister Sledge's "We Are Family" its anthem during its 1979 championship season?

A: Pittsburgh Pirates

HALL OF FAMER ERNIE BANKS WAS KNOWN AS "MR. _____."

Answer: Cub

MATCH TEAMS WITH MEMORABLE MANAGERS:

1. Dodgers	A. Connie Mack
2. Giants	B. Tommy Lasorda
3. Orioles	C. Earl Weaver
4. A's	D. John McGraw

Answers: 1-B, 2-D, 3-C, 4-A

Q: In what year did divisional play begin?

A: 1969

ASTROTURF IS GETTING UPROOTED AT BIG LEAGUE STADIUMS. ALL BUT ONE OF THE FOLLOWING PARKS FEATURE NATURAL GRASS:

A. Kauffman Stadium (Royals)
B. New Comiskey Park (White Sox)
C. Mile High Stadium (Rockies)
D. Riverfront Stadium (Reds)
E. Candlestick Park (Giants)

Answer: D

BETWEEN BEING PHILADELPHIA'S TEAM AND BEING OAKLAND'S TEAM, THE A'S DID A STINT IN _____.

Answer: Kansas City (1955–67)

Q: What team features a running man with a baseball for a head as part of its logo?

A: Cincinnati Reds

TRUE OR FALSE:

No AL team has both stayed in the same city and kept the same name through all the years since the league's founding in 1901.

Answer: False

Extra Bases>

The lone exception is the Detroit Tigers.

DURING ITS BOSTON YEARS, THE BRAVES FRANCHISE ALSO WENT BY ALL BUT ONE OF THE FOLLOWING NAMES:

A. Bees
B. Beaneaters
C. Doves
D. Clippers
E. Rustlers

Answer: D

True or False:

The 1899 Cleveland Spiders (NL) were one of the worst teams ever.

Answer: True

Extra Bases>

The Spiders were 20–134; they closed out their season by going 1–40.

PLAYERS

Q: What was the first father–son duo to play in the big leagues at the same time?

A: Ken Griffey and Ken Griffey Jr.

Extra Bases> Opening Day 1989 found Griffey Sr. playing for the Reds and "Junior" with the Mariners. Pops joined the Mariners in 1990. Then, on September 14, 1990, Griffey Sr. and Jr. hit back-to-back homers in a game against the Angels.

True or False:

Dodgers pitcher Hideo Nomo is the first Japanese player to make the American big leagues.

Answer: False

Extra Bases> Masanori Murakami was a relief pitcher for the Giants during the 1964–65 seasons.

What elite club includes Cecil Fielder, George Foster, and Hank Greenberg?

A. Hall of Fame
B. batting title winners
C. players who have achieved 50-homer seasons
D. Detroit Tigers stars over the years
E. Elks

Answer: C

Extra Bases> Herewith, their big seasons: Fielder, 51 homers for the Tigers in 1990; Foster, 52 homers for the '77 Reds; and Greenberg, 58 homers for the '38 Tigers.

BESIDES BASEBALL, WHAT IS THE OTHER PROFESSIONAL PURSUIT OF THESE TWO-SPORT MEN:

1. Danny Ainge
2. Bo Jackson
3. Jack Clark
4. Robin Yount

A. golf
B. basketball
C. football
D. drag racing

Answers: 1-B, 2-C, 3-D, 4-A

IN 1982, THE CARDINALS AND PADRES SWAPPED STAR SHORT-STOPS, WITH ______ GOING TO ST. LOUIS FOR ______.

Answers: Ozzie Smith, Garry Templeton

WHO IS THE OLDEST PLAYER TO WIN A HOME RUN TITLE?

A. Dave Winfield
B. Darrell Evans
C. Mike Schmidt
D. Hank Aaron
E. Jeff Burroughs

Answer: B

Extra Bases> Evans hit 40 for the Tigers in 1985, at the age of thirty-eight.

True or False:

A player on a last-place team has never been named MVP.

Answer: False

Extra Bases>

Outfielder Andre Dawson won the award in 1987, when he hit 49 HRs and drove in 137 runs for the cellar-dwelling Cubs.

Q: What Tigers star of the '70s was discovered in Michigan's Jackson State Prison?

A: Ron LeFlore

Extra Bases>

LeFlore was serving 5 to 15 years for armed robbery. Fittingly, he would make his mark in the majors as a base stealer.

WHAT WAS ESPECIALLY IMPRESSIVE ABOUT JEFF BAGWELL'S 1994 NUMBERS (.368, 39 HRS, 116 RBIS)?

A. Bagwell was coming off a .268, 19 HR, 84 RBI season.

B. He put up these numbers during a strike-shortened season.

C. The Astros team he played for only won 46 games.

D. Bagwell was coming back from hip replacement surgery.

E. It was Bagwell's rookie season.

Answer: B

Extra Bases> Bagwell did all his damage in just 400 at bats.

MATCH PLAYERS AND POSITIONS:

1. Roberto Alomar	A. first baseman
2. Dave Justice	B. second baseman
3. Frank Thomas	C. third baseman
4. Matt Williams	D. outfielder

Answers: 1-B, 2-D, 3-A, 4-C

For the '78 Yankees, Ron Guidry was nearly unbeatable, going 25– _____ with a 1.74 ERA.

Answer: 3

True or False:

Carlos Baerga is the first and only player to homer from each side of the plate in a single inning.

Answer: True

Extra Bases>

The Indians second baseman managed the feat on April 8, 1993.

Q: Who is the most recent pitcher to win 30 games in a season?

A: Denny McLain (31–6, 1.96 ERA for the Tigers in '68)

MATCH UP BIG-LEAGUE SIBLINGS:

1. Paul and
2. Jim and
3. Mike and
4. Ken and

A. Graig Nettles
B. George Brett
C. Dizzy Dean
D. Greg Maddux

Answers: 1-C, 2-A, 3-D, 4-B

ALL BUT ONE OF THE FOLLOWING APPLY TO MOE BERG:

A. journeyman catcher
B. proficient in several foreign languages
C. law school graduate
D. inventor of the camera flashbulb
E. World War II spy

Answer: D

PITCHERS FOSTER, FISCHER, MARQUAND, AND WADDELL SHARE THE NICKNAME _____.

Answer: Rube

True or False:

In 1995, Atlanta's Greg Maddux became the first pitcher ever to win the Cy Young Award four straight seasons.

Answer: True

In 1961, Norm Cash hit .361 with 41 homers and 132 RBIs, yet finished fourth in the MVP balloting. Why?

A. Sportswriters didn't like him.
B. His season was marred by several ugly brawls.
C. It's questionable whether someone deserves an MVP if his team finishes in the cellar.
D. Simple. It was 1961, a banner year for several other players, including Roger Maris and Jim Gentile.
E. He was an abominable defensive player.

Answer: D

Q: What basketball superstar took a crack at making the White Sox?

A: Michael Jordan

JIM EISENREICH SUFFERS FROM _____, A NERVOUS DISORDER CHARACTERIZED BY UNCONTROLLABLE TICS. THE AFFLICTION FORCED HIM TO QUIT AFTER JUST A FEW SEASONS WITH THE TWINS. HE WAS OUT OF BASEBALL FOR SEVERAL YEARS, BUT THEN HE MADE A HEROIC COMEBACK WITH THE ROYALS AND PHILLIES.

Answer: Tourette's syndrome

True or False:

Dwight Gooden was the youngest 20-game winner in baseball history.

Answer: True

Extra Bases>

Gooden was only 20 in 1985, when he went 24–4, with a 1.53 ERA and 268 strikeouts.

What honors did Tigers reliever Willie Hernandez collect in 1984?

A. named an All-Star
B. Cy Young Award
C. MVP
D. all of the above
E. none of the above

Answer: D

Extra Bases>

Hernandez was 9–3 with 32 saves and a 1.92 ERA.

Q: Who was NL MVP in 1990, '92, and '93?

A: Barry Bonds (Pirates)

MATCH UP SECOND BASEMEN WITH SHORTSTOPS TO FORM CLASSIC DOUBLE-PLAY COMBOS:

1. Lou Whitaker
2. Nellie Fox
3. Joe Morgan
4. Bobby Grich

A. Alan Trammell
B. Dave Concepcion
C. Luis Aparacio
D. Mark Belanger

Answers: 1-A, 2-C, 3-B, 4-D

THROWING OUT BASE RUNNERS FROM HIS KNEES IS THE TRADEMARK OF ______, A GOLD GLOVE CATCHER WHO'S SEEN ACTION WITH THE PADRES AND MARLINS.

Answer: Benito Santiago

Q: Who is the only player to be named both Rookie of the Year and MVP of the same season?

A: Fred Lynn

Extra Bases>

In his spectacular debut season, Lynn batted .331 with 21 homers and 105 RBIs, and won a Gold Glove for his play in center field.

TRUE OR FALSE:

Blue Jays pitcher Dave Stieb once threw three one-hitters in four starts.

Answer: True

How is it possible that Herb Washington appeared in 104 games for the A's in the 1974–75 season without pitching or recording an at bat?

A. He was used solely as a defensive replacement.

B. He was used solely as a bunter, so he never recorded at bats.

C. He was the team's designated pinch runner.

D. He was a light-hitting shortstop, so the A's let the pitcher bat and assigned the DH to hit for him.

E. That's easy—he was the third-base coach.

Answer: C

Extra Bases> Washington was a former track star who could neither pitch nor hit nor field. But he could steal bases—30 of them all told.

On September 26, 1908, Chicago's Ed Reulbach set a record by pitching ______ in both games of a doubleheader against the Dodgers.

Answer: shutouts

Q: What pitcher tossed a perfect game through twelve innings, only to lose in the thirteenth?

A: Harvey Haddix

Extra Bases> Haddix was virtually untouchable against the Braves on May 26, 1959. Sadly, his Pirates teammates couldn't muster any offense either, and the score stood at 0–0 going into the bottom of the thirteenth. It was then that the Braves collected their only hit, a game-winning homer by Joe Adcock.

TRUE OR FALSE:

Kirby Puckett didn't hit any homers during his rookie season.

Answer: True

Extra Bases> Amazingly, the Twins center fielder went dingerless in 557 at bats in 1984. He had just four in 691 at bats the following year. Then, Puckett exploded, racking up totals of 31, 28, and 24 homers the next three seasons.

THE 1971 ORIOLES FEATURED FOUR 20-GAME WINNERS. WHO WAS NOT IN THAT SELECT GROUP?

A. Jim Palmer
B. Steve Stone
C. Mike Cuellar
D. Pat Dobson
E. Dave McNally

Answer: B

MANNY MOTA, SMOKY BURGESS, STEVE BRAUN, AND MIKE LUM ALL MADE THEIR MARK AS ______ HITTERS.

Answer: pinch

Q: What player set the stage for free agency by mounting a 1970 legal challenge to baseball's reserve clause, which allowed teams to trade players at their whim?

A: Curt Flood (Cardinals outfielder)

MATCH UP COLORFUL BASEBALL NAMES:

1. Lu
2. Mordecai "Three Finger"
3. Dallas
4. Dolly

A. Green
B. Gray
C. Blue
D. Brown

Answers: 1-C, 2-D, 3-A, 4-B

IN 1981, DODGER ROOKIE SENSATION ______ WON HIS FIRST TEN DECISIONS AND PITCHED SHUTOUTS IN FIVE OF HIS FIRST SEVEN STARTS.

Answer: Fernando Valenzuela

Q: What 1994 baseball movie featured cameos by such real-life players as Ken Griffey Jr., Wally Joyner, and Rafael Palmeiro?

A: *Little Big League*

True or False:

Bob Feller was seventeen when he joined the Indians in 1936, making him the youngest big leaguer of the twentieth century.

Answer: False

Extra Bases> In 1944, baseball's talent pool was seriously depleted by World War II—so much so that the Dodgers called up 15-year-old Joe Nuxhall. In order to play, Nuxhall required a note of permission from his high school principal.

Felipe, Jesus, and Matty _____ made an appearance as the first-ever all-brother outfield, for the Giants in 1963. It was just for one inning, as it required Willie Mays to sit on the bench.

Answer: Alou

Q: Who is the charter member of the "40/40 club"—40 homers, 40 stolen bases in the same season?

A: Jose Canseco (A's, 1988)

Playoffs and World Series

In the opener of the '82 Fall Classic, Milwaukee's ______ became the first player ever to collect five hits in a Series game.

Answer: Paul Molitor

Extra Bases> Molitor went 5 for 6, teammate Robin Yount went 4 for 6, as the Brewers trounced the Cardinals, 10–0.

GAME FOUR OF THE 1941 SERIES CAME DOWN TO A:

A. balk by the pitcher
B. dropped third strike by the catcher
C. steal of home
D. hit batsman with the bases loaded
E. dropped foul pop-up

Answer: B

Extra Bases> With two outs in the ninth inning and Brooklyn up, 4–3, catcher Mickey Owen dropped a third strike on Tommy Henrich of the Yankees. Henrich reached first and the Yankees rallied for a 7–4 victory. The Yankees went on to win the Series.

TRUE OR FALSE:

The '87 Twins-Cardinals matchup featured the first Series game ever played indoors.

Answer: True

Q: Who is the only pitcher to throw a perfect game (no hits, no walks, no nothin') in a World Series?

A: Don Larsen

Extra Bases>

Larsen set down 27 straight Dodgers on October 8, 1956. The Yankees won Game Five, 2–0.

MATCH UP WORLD SERIES OUTCOMES:

1. Blue Jays, 4-2, over
2. Giants swept by
3. Red Sox lose in seven to
4. Twins lose in seven to

A. A's in 1989
B. Phillies in 1993
C. Dodgers in 1965
D. Mets in 1986

Answers: 1-B, 2-A, 3-D, 4-C

What is Bill Wambsganss's contribution to World Series history?

A. He hit the first homer in a Series.
B. He was the first pitcher to throw a no-hitter in the Fall Classic.
C. He struck out with the bases loaded to end the 1959 Series.
D. As baseball commissioner, he dreamed up the concept.
E. He turned the first and only unassisted triple play in a Series.

Answer: E

Extra Bases> Wambsganss, a second baseman for the Indians, turned the trick in Game Five of the 1920 Series against the Dodgers.

A GHOSTWRITTEN NEWSPAPER COLUMN CARRYING METS PITCHER _____'S BYLINE WAS CRITICAL OF RIVAL HURLERS OREL HERSHISER AND JAY HOWELL. IT INADVERTENTLY SERVED TO FIRE UP THE DODGERS IN THE 1988 PLAYOFFS.

Answer: Dave Cone

Q: Who holds the record for consecutive hits in the World Series?

A: Billy Hatcher

Extra Bases>

He had seven straight for the Reds in the 1990 Series against the A's.

True or False:

Rod Carew, Harry Heilmann, Ferguson Jenkins, Ted Lyons, and Billy Williams are among the notable players that never got to play in a World Series.

Answer: True

Which is the first team to sweep in both the league playoffs and the World Series?

A. 1969 Mets
B. 1976 Reds
C. 1979 Yankees
D. 1984 Tigers
E. 1992 Blue Jays

Answer: B

Extra Bases> The Reds dispensed with the Phillies in three and the Yankees in four.

A 1908 baserunning error by _____ is one of the most notorious events in baseball history. The 19-year-old Giants rookie headed straight for the dugout following a game-winning hit, failing to touch second in the process. Cubs second baseman Johnny Evers called for the ball and stepped on the base, negating the winning run. Because fans were romping about the field, oblivious to the Giants' sudden change of fate, the game had to be replayed. The Giants and Cubs finished the season tied, meaning the replay was effectively a playoff game. This time the Cubs won, clinching the pennant.

Answer: Fred Merkle

Q: Who hit a dramatic three-run homer to clinch a Yankee win, 5–4, over the Red Sox in a 1978 divisional playoff game?

A: Bucky Dent

TRUE OR FALSE:

When the Phillies beat the Royals in 1980, it was the first Series win in the team's 98-year history.

Answer: True

Match up classic World Series catches:

1. Sandy Amoros — A. pulled in Vic Wertz's 430-foot drive
2. Al Gionfriddo — B. ran down a towering Yogi Berra blast
3. Willie Mays — C. dove to catch a Brooks Robinson liner
4. Ron Swoboda — D. corralled a 415-foot shot by Joe DiMaggio

Answers: 1-B, 2-D, 3-A, 4-C

Extra Bases> Gionfriddo's grab clinched a Dodger victory over the Yankees in Game Six of the '47 Series. The over-the-shoulder catch Mays made in Game One of the '54 Series against the Indians is often considered the most spectacular play ever. With the tying runs on base, Amoros's catch in 1955 preserved a 2–0 lead and helped clinch a World Series win for the Dodgers in their eighth meeting with their crosstown rivals, the Yankees. Swoboda's heroics put Game Four of the '69 Series into extra innings, where the Miracle Mets bested the Orioles.

Which Series-winning team was dubbed "The Hitless Wonders"?

A. 1957 Braves
B. 1970 Orioles
C. 1906 White Sox
D. 1940 Reds
E. 1916 Red Sox

Answer: C

Extra Bases> The team batted a combined .230; Lee Tannehill, who often hit cleanup, batted just .183 for the year.

PITCHER ______ WAS A PERFECT 6–0 IN WORLD SERIES APPEARANCES, WHILE ______ WAS A PERFECTLY AWFUL 0–7 IN PLAYOFF DECISIONS.

Answer: Lefty Gomez (Yankees), Jerry Reuss (Pirates, Dodgers)

True or False:

The first World Series was played in 1900.

Answer: False

Extra Bases> The Fall Classic was inaugurated in 1903, with the Boston Pilgrims beating the Pirates, five games to three (it was a best-of-nine format).

Q: Who is the only player to be caught stealing for the last out in a World Series?

A: Babe Ruth

Extra Bases> Bottom of the ninth, Game Seven of the 1926 Series, the Bambino was gunned down trying to steal second by Cardinal catcher Bob O'Farrell.

WHEN WAS THE FIRST TELEVISED WORLD SERIES?

A. 1928
B. 1936
C. 1940
D. 1947
E. 1954

Answer: D

Extra Bases> Yankees and Dodgers was the matchup; Ford and Gillette were the official sponsors.

On October 20, 1993, the Blue Jays rallied past the _____, 15–14, in the highest-scoring World Series game ever.

Answer: Philadelphia Phillies

True or False:

Yankees star Willie Randolph hit a dramatic ninth-inning homer to clinch the '76 playoffs over the Royals.

Answer: False

Extra Bases>

It was hit by Chris Chambliss.

Match up classic World Series pitching duels:

1. Denny McLain	A. Sandy Koufax
2. Whitey Ford	B. John Smoltz
3. Jack Morris	C. Bob Gibson
4. Bob Feller	D. Johnny Sain

Answers: 1-C, 2-A, 3-B, 4-D

Extra Bases> Boston's Sain outdueled Cleveland's Feller, 1–0, in the opener of the '48 Series; Koufax of the Dodgers beat Ford of the Yankees in both the first and fourth games of the '63 Series; in the '68 Series opener, St. Louis's Gibson struck out 17 while besting Detroit's McLain, 4–0; Morris outdueled Atlanta's Smoltz, 1–0, to clinch the '91 Series for the Twins.

Q: Who is the only player to appear in the World Series with four different teams?

A: Lonnie Smith

Extra Bases> Lonnie was lucky enough to be with the Phillies in '80, Cardinals in '82, Royals in '85, and Braves in '91 and '92.

In the '47 Series, what pinch hitter broke up Yankee pitcher Floyd Beven's no-hit bid with two outs in the bottom of the ninth?

A. Dusty Rhodes
B. Minnie Minoso
C. Cookie Lavagetto
D. Andy Pafko
E. Mike Ivie

Answer: C

Extra Bases> Because Bevens had been wild all day, when Lavagetto came to the plate the Yankee hurler had a no-hitter, but not a shutout. The score stood at 2–1 and there were two runners on base. Lavagetto hit a double, driving in the runners and giving the Dodgers a 3–2 win.

In the opening game of the 1988 Series, injured Dodger outfielder ______ was called upon to pinch-hit with two outs in the bottom of the ninth. He limped to the plate, then proceeded to reach A's relief ace Dennis Eckersley for a game-winning homer.

Answer: Kirk Gibson

True or False:

There has never been an all-Chicago World Series.

Answer: False

Extra Bases> In 1906, the White Sox bested the Cubs, four games to two.

Q: The Royals won their division 1976–78, only to lose to what team in the playoffs?

A: Yankees

Extra Bases> But the Royals finally got their revenge by beating the Yankees for the 1980 pennant.

WHO HOLDS A RECORD FOR HAVING PITCHED 22⅓ CONSECUTIVE SCORELESS INNINGS IN THE PLAYOFFS?

A. Dave Stewart
B. John Smoltz
C. Mike Torrez
D. Steve Avery
E. John Tudor

Answer: D (Braves)

PITTSBURGH SECOND BASEMAN _____ HOMERED OFF RALPH TERRY IN THE BOTTOM OF THE NINTH OF GAME SEVEN TO CARRY THE PIRATES PAST THE YANKEES FOR THE 1960 WORLD CHAMPIONSHIP.

Answer: Bill Mazeroski

True or False:

Three errors by the same player in the same inning is the World Series record.

Answer: True

Extra Bases>

Dodger outfielder Willie Davis came unglued during the fifth inning of Game Two of the 1966 Series.

WHO ARE THE ONLY BROTHERS TO HOMER IN THE SAME WORLD SERIES GAME?

A. Joe and Dom DiMaggio
B. Ed and Chuck Brinkman
C. Fred and Josh Clarke
D. Jose and Hector Cruz
E. Clete and Ken Boyer

Answer: E

Extra Bases>

Ken connected for the Cardinals, brother Clete answered two innings later for the Yankees in Game Seven of the '64 Series.

Q: What player earned the nickname "Mr. October" for his playoff and World Series heroics?

A: Reggie Jackson

Extra Bases> Playing for the Yankees in 1977, Jackson managed his most memorable October feat: three straight homers on three straight pitches in Game Six to clinch a World Series win over the Dodgers.

THE 1989 SERIES BETWEEN THE A'S AND GIANTS WAS DELAYED FOR TEN DAYS DUE TO _____.

Answer: an earthquake

TRUE OR FALSE:

Babe Ruth holds the all-time record for World Series homers.

Answer: False

Extra Bases>

The record belongs to Mickey Mantle, who hit 18 round trippers in ten Fall Classics.

Q: What is the name of the pinch hitter who delivered a two-out, bases loaded single in the 1992 playoffs to carry Atlanta past the Pirates?

A: Francisco Cabrera

IN 1975, RED SOX CATCHER CARLTON FISK HIT ONE OF THE MOST DRAMATIC SERIES HOMERS EVER. WHICH OF THE FOLLOWING POINTS IS PURE BALDERDASH:

A. It almost hooked foul.
B. Fisk electrified the fans by waving his arms wildly, urging the ball to stay fair.
C. It struck the foul pole.
D. The homer carried the Red Sox past the Reds, 7–6, in 12 innings.
E. Fisk was mobbed by fans and required a police escort to round the bases.

Answer: E

THE 1991 SERIES BETWEEN THE BRAVES AND TWINS WAS THE FIRST TO CONTAIN THREE _____ GAMES.

Answer: extra-inning

Q: What is the only city to be represented in the World Series ten straight years?

A: New York City

Extra Bases> From 1949 to 1958, the World Series was a Big Apple affair. With the Yankees making it nine times, Dodgers five, and Giants twice, fully 16 of 20 Series slots were occupied by "New Yawk" teams.

Match up World Series nicknames:

1. Subway Series
2. I-70 Series
3. Bay Series
4. Trolley Series

A. Royals vs. Cardinals, 1985

B. Giants vs. A's, 1989

C. Cardinals vs. Browns, 1944

D. Yankees vs. Mets, unlikely matchup touted by sportswriters every April

Answers: 1-D, 2-A, 3-B, 4-C

True or False:

The longest World Series hitting streak lasted 17 games.

Answer: True

Extra Bases>

Yankees outfielder Hank Bauer owns the streak, which spanned the 1956 to the 1958 Fall Classics.

WHICH OF THE FOLLOWING TEAMS DID NOT PARTICIPATE IN POST-SEASON PLAY AT LEAST THREE YEARS IN A ROW?

A. Cardinals, 1942–44
B. Tigers, 1966–68
C. Orioles, 1969–71
D. A's, 1971–74
E. Yankees, 1976–78

Answer: B

IMMORTALS

ALL BUT ONE OF THE FOLLOWING HAS MANAGED A TRIPLE-CROWN SEASON (LEADING THE LEAGUE IN BATTING AVERAGE, HOMERS, AND RBIs):

A. Frank Robinson
B. Ted Williams
C. Carl Yastrzemski
D. Hank Greenberg
E. Jimmie Foxx

Answer: D

Extra Bases> Herewith, the four players' awesome triple crown numbers: Foxx—.356, 48 HRs, 163 RBIs for the A's in 1933; Robinson—.316, 49 HRs, 122 RBIs for the Orioles in 1966; Yastrzemski—.326, 44 HRs, 121 RBIs for the Red Sox in 1967. Fellow Red Sox great Williams managed two triple crowns: in 1942—.356, 36 homers, 137 RBIs and 1947—.343, 32 HRs, 114 RBIs. Tigers slugger Greenberg led the league in both homers and RBIs on three separate occasions, but each time failed to win the third leg of the triple crown—the batting title.

Q: Who is the only pitcher to win Cy Young awards in both leagues?

A: Gaylord Perry

TRUE OR FALSE:

Ralph Kiner has the all-time best ratio for homers to at bats.

Answer: False

Extra Bases>

Ruth was tops, but Kiner homered every 14.1 at bats, good for second best.

MATCH UP CLASSIC BATTERIES (PITCHERS AND CATCHERS):

1. Steve Carlton
2. Christy Mathewson
3. Don Newcombe
4. Allie Reynolds

A. Yogi Berra
B. Roy Campanella
C. Roger Bresnahan
D. Tim McCarver

Answers: 1-D, 2-C, 3-B, 4-A

THE SPORTING GOODS COMPANY HE FOUNDED IS STILL GOING STRONG, BUT ______ ALSO DISTINGUISHED HIMSELF AS A PITCHER FOR THE BOSTON RED STOCKINGS (NATIONAL ASSOCIATION) AND CHICAGO WHITE STOCKINGS (LATER KNOWN AS THE CUBS). HE BECAME BASEBALL'S FIRST 200-GAME WINNER, RETIRED IN 1878 WITH A 207–56 RECORD, AND WAS INDUCTED INTO THE HALL OF FAME IN 1939.

Answer: Albert Spalding

WHICH OF THE FOLLOWING WAS NOT AMONG THE "FIVE IMMORTALS," THE INITIAL INDUCTEES INTO THE HALL OF FAME?

A. Babe Ruth
B. Rogers Hornsby
C. Honus Wagner
D. Christy Mathewson
E. Ty Cobb

Answer: B

True or False:

Tris Speaker's career doubles tally is higher than Hank Aaron's career homer tally.

Answer: True

Extra Bases>

But it's close: the Hall of Fame center fielder has 793 doubles; Aaron hit 755 homers.

JOHNNY MIZE HOLDS A RECORD FOR HAVING HAD SIX ______ - HOMER GAMES DURING HIS CAREER.

Answer: three

Q: What turn-of-the-century pitcher had a record seven 30-win seasons?

A: Kid Nichols

Extra Bases> Nichols had his big seasons between 1890 and 1898 while pitching for the Boston Beaneaters (NL).

How could someone who never hit more than 12 homers in a season come to be known as Frank "Home Run" Baker?

A. Sarcasm: nobody liked him.
B. For a pitcher, his power was impressive.
C. The name refers to the fact that, as a pitcher, he yielded a ton of dingers.
D. All old-time players had nicknames, and this one just happened to sound good.
E. Baker played during the so-called dead ball era, when the ball was constructed differently and homers were harder to come by.

Answer: E

TRUE OR FALSE:

Though a much-touted phenomenon, Willie Mays's first few professional games were quite inauspicious.

Answer: True

Extra Bases> Mays started off 0 for 12, but then homered off Warren Spahn of the Braves for his first big-league hit. Spahn later said: " . . . I'll never forgive myself. We might have gotten rid of Willie forever if I'd only struck him out."

MANY OF THE RECORDS BELONGING TO INDIANS GREAT BOB FELLER HAVE FALLEN BY THE WAYSIDE, BUT HE REMAINS THE LAST PITCHER TO THROW A NO-HITTER ON _____.

Answer: Opening Day
(versus the White Sox in 1940)

Q: Who wrote an autobiography entitled *Nice Guys Finish Last*?

A: Leo Durocher

MATCH PLAYERS WITH THE GREATS THEY REPLACED:

1. Doug DeCinces
2. Bobby Murcer
3. Ray Knight
4. Greg Brock

A. Pete Rose
B. Brooks Robinson
C. Steve Garvey
D. Mickey Mantle

Answers: 1-B, 2-D, 3-A, 4-C

AMONG CATCHERS, WHO HAD THE HIGHEST SINGLE-SEASON BATTING AVERAGE IN THE TWENTIETH CENTURY?

A. Roy Campanella
B. Bill Dickey
C. Thurman Munson
D. Mike Piazza
E. Carlton Fisk

Answer: B

Extra Bases> Dickey batted .362 with the Yankees in 1936.

True or False:

Charles "Old Hoss" Radbourn managed the NL Providence Grays to a 59–12 record in 1884.

Answer: False

Extra Bases> Actually, that was Radbourn's record as a workhorse pitcher. In 678 innings, he had 441 strikeouts, 98 walks, and a rock-bottom 1.38 ERA.

MAXIMILIAN CARNARIUS WAS THE NAME AT BIRTH OF ______, HALL OF FAME OUTFIELDER FOR THE PIRATES AND DODGERS, 1910–29.

Answer: Max Carey

Q: Where is the baseball Hall of Fame located?

A: Cooperstown, New York

BABE RUTH STARTED HIS CAREER AS A:

A. shortstop
B. first baseman
C. center fielder
D. catcher
E. pitcher

Answer: E

Extra Bases> And he was a damned good one. Ruth racked up a 94–46 lifetime record. He was a two-time 20-game winner for the Red Sox, the team for which he started his career. Even after joining the Yankees, who wanted his bat in the lineup every day and used him as an outfielder, Ruth made five pitching appearances and won them all.

TRUE OR FALSE:

George Kell once won a batting title by 1/10,000th of a point.

Answer: True

Extra Bases>

In 1949, the Tigers Hall of Fame third baseman edged Ted Williams, .3429 to .3428.

DURING THE CALIFORNIA PRIMARY, RIGHT BEFORE HE WAS ASSASSINATED, ROBERT F. KENNEDY DELIVERED A SPEECH IN WHICH HE CONGRATULATED ______ ON THROWING SIX CONSECUTIVE SHUTOUTS.

Answer: Don Drysdale (Dodgers in '68)

Q: Who was the first NL player to reach the 500-homer plateau?

A: Mel Ott

Extra Bases>

The Giants great hit 511 homers during a career that spanned 1926–47.

MATCH PLAYERS WITH BOASTS:

1. "I'm the straw that stirs the drink."
2. "It ain't bragging if you can do it."
3. "I don't like to sound egotistical, but every time I stepped to the plate with a bat in my hands, I couldn't help but feel sorry for the pitcher."
4. "Most guys would rather wear a hamburger suit in a lion's den than deal with me."

A. Rogers Hornsby
B. Reggie Jackson
C. Dave Parker
D. Dizzy Dean

Answers: 1-B, 2-D, 3-A, 4-C

WHAT INNOVATION DID RAY SCHALK, A HALL OF FAME WHITE SOX CATCHER, BRING TO HIS POSITION?

A. He invented hand signals for calling pitches.
B. He was the first to wear shin guards.
C. He was the first to wear a face mask.
D. He was the first to back up plays at first and third base.
E. He was the first catcher that squatted down to receive pitches.

Answer: D

PIRATE'S OUTFIELDER PAUL WANER WAS A ______ HITTER IN EACH OF HIS FIRST 12 SEASONS, 1926–37.

Answer: .300

True or False:

There are no umpires in the Hall of Fame.

Answer: False

Extra Bases> Along with players, the Hall also features managers, sportswriters, executives, and umpires. Among the notable men in blue: Jocko Conlan, Cal Hubbard, and William Klem.

Q: Who broke the "color barrier" in baseball?

A: Jackie Robinson

Extra Bases> Robinson joined the Brooklyn Dodgers in 1947, and showed quiet heroism in the face of racial prejudice from both fans and opposing players. Dodger GM Branch Rickey had cautioned Robinson that he would face extraordinary pressures and would have to possess "the guts not to fight back." Robinson let his play speak for itself, and earned Rookie of the Year honors in 1947 with a .297 batting average and league-leading 29 stolen bases.

What is Ty Cobb's lifetime batting average?

A. .301
B. .323
C. .344
D. .366
E. .397

Answer: D

Extra Bases> Cobb started out with the Tigers in 1905, retired from the Philadelphia A's in 1928, and in the interim won 12 batting titles, and put up the highest lifetime average ever.

During the 1950s, New Yorkers were treated to some fine center fielding. Each of the city's major league teams had a future Hall of Famer in that position. The Big Three were: _____, _____, and _____.

Answer: Willie Mays (Giants), Mickey Mantle (Yankees), and Duke Snider (Dodgers)

TRUE OR FALSE:

Roberto Clemente decided to retire as soon as he collected his 3,000th hit.

Answer: False

Extra Bases> The Pirate great finished up the 1972 season with exactly 3,000 hits. But tragedy prevented him from coming back for more: Clemente was killed in a plane crash on New Year's Eve, while trying to bring relief supplies to victims of an earthquake in Nicaragua.

Q: What Hall of Fame pitcher didn't record his first win until age thirty-one?

A: Dazzy Vance

Extra Bases> Vance made his first big-league appearance for the Pirates in 1915. But his first win didn't come until seven years later with the Dodgers. Still, by the time Vance's career ended in 1935 he was 197–140 and destined for Cooperstown.

WHAT TWO PLAYERS COMBINED FOR THE MOST HOMERS AS TEAMMATES?

A. Babe Ruth and Lou Gehrig
B. Willie Mays and Willie McCovey
C. Mike Schmidt and Greg Luzinski
D. Hank Aaron and Eddie Mathews
E. Duane Kuiper and Bert Campaneris

Answer: D (863 homers as Braves teammates)

DURING BOB FELLER'S 1940 OPENING DAY NO-NO, _____, A STAR SHORTSTOP FOR THE WHITE SOX AND CONTACT-HITTER EXTRAORDINAIRE, UPPED THE SUSPENSE BY FOULING OFF 15 PITCHES IN ONE PLATE APPEARANCE.

Answer: Luke Appling

MATCH NICKNAMES TO PLAYERS:

1. "Big Train"	A. Joe Medwick
2. "Say Hey Kid"	B. Walter Johnson
3. "Ducky"	C. Ty Cobb
4. "Georgia Peach"	D. Willie Mays

Answers: 1-B, 2-D, 3-A, 4-C

TRUE OR FALSE:

In the 1934 All-Star Game, Giants hurler Carl Hubbell struck out five future Hall of Famers in a row.

Answer: True

Extra Bases>

Hubbell KO'd Babe Ruth, Lou Gehrig, Jimmie Foxx, Al Simmons, and Joe Cronin.

How many no-hitters did Nolan Ryan throw during his career?

A. 0
B. 2
C. 4
D. 7
E. 10

Answer: D

ACE RELIEVER ______ WAS ALSO KNOWN FOR HIS DISTINCTIVE HANDLEBAR MUSTACHE.

Answer: Rollie Fingers

TRUE OR FALSE:

Paddy Driscoll, George Halas, Greasy Neale, and Jim Thorpe are all members of baseball's Hall of Fame.

Answer: False

Extra Bases>

All played big-league ball, but really distinguished themselves on the gridiron, and are members of football's Hall of Fame.

BESIDES TY COBB AND ROGERS HORNSBY, ______ IS THE ONLY PLAYER TO BAT .400 THREE TIMES.

Answer: Jesse Burkett

Extra Bases>

Burkett was a star outfielder for the NL's Cleveland Spiders during the 1890s. He was inducted into the Hall of Fame in 1946.

Q: Who is the Tigers all-time leader in games played and homers?

A: Al Kaline

Extra Bases>

Kaline played in 2,834 games and hit 399 homers; he was elected into the Hall of Fame in 1980.

LORE AND LINGO

TRUE OR FALSE:

Abner Doubleday invented the game of baseball.

Answer: False

Extra Bases> Doubleday is often credited, and the "Doubleday Baseball," now on display at the Hall of Fame, acts as Exhibit A. Better evidence supports the notion that Alexander Cartwright invented the game.

MATCH CLASSIC HOMERS WITH THEIR AUTHORS:

1. "The Called Shot"
2. "Homer in the Gloamin'"
3. "Shot Heard 'Round the World"
4. "Bunt Home Run"

A. Leo Durocher
B. Bobby Thomson
C. Babe Ruth
D. Gabby Hartnett

Answers: 1-C, 2-D, 3-B, 4-A

Extra Bases> The Babe's "Called Shot" in the '32 Series was reputedly hit to the exact spot in the bleachers where he had pointed a moment earlier; Thomson's "Shot" on October 3, 1951, gave the Giants the pennant over their crosstown rivals, the Brooklyn Dodgers; Hartnett's "Homer in the Gloamin" was hit September 28, 1938, just as darkness fell on Wrigley, and carried the Cubs past the Pirates into first place; Durocher's famous homer was actually a comedy of errors that allowed him to circle the bases on a bunt during the 1938 All-Star Game.

Q: What is manufactured by the Hillerich & Bradsby Company?

A: Louisville Slugger baseball bats

WHY WAS THERE "NO JOY IN MUDVILLE"?

A. The city's professional franchise folded.
B. Blue Laws banned Sunday baseball.
C. Casey struck out.
D. George Steinbrenner purchased the team.
E. There were interminable rain delays.

Answer: C

Extra Bases> Ernest Thayer's classic poem, "Casey At The Bat," first appeared in the June 3, 1888, edition of the *San Francisco Examiner*. It ends with this memorable stanza: "Oh! somewhere in this favored land the sun is shining bright; The band is playing somewhere, and somewhere hearts are light, and somewhere men are laughing, and somewhere children shout; But there is no joy in Mudville—mighty Casey has struck out."

In 1934, Giants manager Bill Terry made his famous quip: "Is _____ still in the league?" The slighted team got sweet revenge, playing spoiler and knocking the Giants out of the pennant race.

Answer: Brooklyn

True or False:

A number of big-league second basemen and shortstops hail from the town of San Pedro de Macoris in the Dominican Republic.

Answer: True

Extra Bases>

Among them: Tony Fernandez and Juan Castillo.

Q: Who was famed for the batting strategy, "Hit 'em where they ain't"?

A: Wee Willie Keeler

WHAT WAS THE STORY WITH "BLIND RYNE" DUREN?

A. He was the first umpire to wear glasses.
B. A fireballing Yankees reliever, he wore Coke-bottle glasses to correct 20/200 vision in one eye.
C. He was a turn-of-the-century A's catcher who simply chose to ignore base stealers.
D. This Reds outfielder got into the practice of crouching down and shielding his head with his hands after losing balls in the sun.
E. He was an Expos linebacker and real-life model for the movie *Blind Duren.*

Answer: B

On May 24, 1935, the Reds hosted the Phillies for baseball's first ______ game.

Answer: night

TRUE OR FALSE:

Pirates announcer Jim Rooker walked from Philadelphia to Pittsburgh in 1987.

Answer: True

Extra Bases> With the Pirates up 10–0, Rooker stated: "If the Bucs blow this one, I'll walk back to Pittsburgh." Sure enough, they did, by a score of 15–11. Numerous fans called demanding that he make good on his word. Rooker decided to make the best of it, raised $81,000 in cash pledges for charity, and set off on a 315-mile jaunt.

Q: What song traditionally is sung by the fans during the seventh-inning stretch?

A: "Take Me Out to the Ball Game"

MATCH PLAYERS WITH SPECIALTIES:

1. Vince Coleman
2. Dave Kingman
3. J. R. Richard
4. Frank White

A. slugger
B. fireballer
C. defensive whiz
D. speedster

Answer: 1-D, 2-A, 3-B, 4-C

"A FAT TUB OF GOO," WAS TALK-SHOW HOST DAVID LETTERMAN'S MEMORABLE DESCRIPTION OF WHAT PLAYER?

A. Cecil Fielder
B. Ivan Rodriguez
C. Mark Portugal
D. Terry Forster
E. Randy Johnson

Answer: D

AT EBBETS FIELD, HOME OF THE BROOKLYN DODGERS, THE SCOREBOARD FEATURED A FAMOUS AD FOR ABE STARK THAT PROMISED: "HIT SIGN, WIN ______."

Answer: suit

True or False:

Bid McPhee, a nineteenth-century star second baseman for the Reds, insisted on fielding bare-handed well into the ballglove era.

Answer: True

Q: What team was famously derided as "First in war, first in peace, and last in the American League"?

A: Washington Senators

WHAT IS THE SIGNIFICANCE OF WALLY PIPP'S TAKING A DAY OFF IN 1925 DUE TO A HEADACHE?

A. The Cardinals ace missed Game Seven of the World Series.

B. Lou Gehrig took his job away and proceeded to play in 2,130 consecutive games.

C. The Pirates lost patience with their moody star, and he became the first baseball player ever given his unconditional release.

D. He became the first player ever placed on the disabled list.

E. Eddie Watkins, the Browns player who subbed for Pipp in center field for the May 12 contest, was hit in the head with a beer bottle and suffered a concussion.

Answer: B

IN 1860, THE BROOKLYN EXCELSIORS EMBARKED ON BASEBALL'S FIRST ______, TRAVELING TO ALBANY, TROY, BUFFALO, ROCHESTER, AND NEWBURGH OVER A TEN-DAY PERIOD.

Answer: road trip

MATCH UP EACH SLANG TERM WITH ITS MEANING:

1. whiff	A. home run
2. muff	B. to hit a batter with a pitch
3. tater	C. to make an error
4. plunk	D. to strike out

Answers: 1-D, 2-C, 3-A, 4-B

TRUE OR FALSE:

The "Gashouse Gang" is the nickname for the great Brooklyn Dodgers teams of the '50s.

Answer: False

Extra Bases>

The nickname belongs to the '30s-era Cardinals, which featured such stars as Rip Collins, Dizzy Dean, Pepper Martin, and Ducky Medwick.

Q: What long-time baseball announcer has as his signature call: "It could be. It might be. It is! A home run!"

A: Harry Caray

WHAT PITCHER RELIED ON AN INNOVATION DUBBED THE "EEPHUS PITCH"?

A. Luis Tiant
B. Rip Sewell
C. Tug McGraw
D. Babe Adams
E. Billy Eephus

Answer: B

Extra Bases> Sewell's trademark was a slow, blooping pitch, sometimes tossed more than 20 feet in the air.

THE FAMOUS TURN-OF-THE-CENTURY CUBS DOUBLE-PLAY SEQUENCE WAS TINKERS TO EVERS TO _____.

Answer: Chance

Match up player names and positions from "Who's on First," Abbott & Costello's classic comedy routine:

1. What
2. I Don't Know
3. I Don't Give a Darn
4. Who

A. first baseman
B. second baseman
C. shortstop
D. third baseman

Answers: 1-B, 2-D, 3-C, 4-A

TRUE OR FALSE:

When Shoeless Joe Jackson was accused of taking part in a gambling scheme that rigged the outcome of the 1919 World Series, White Sox owner Charles Comiskey instructed him to simply: "Say it ain't so, Joe."

Answer: False

Extra Bases> According to legend, as Jackson left the courthouse, a little boy ran up and shouted the now famous line.

Q: Who said, "Don't look back. Something might be gaining on you"?

A: Satchel Paige

Extra Bases> Paige was a star pitcher in the Negro Leagues, who wound up his career with the Indians and Browns. He surfaced one final time with the Kansas City A's in 1965. In response to endless questions about his real age, Paige tossed out a number of sly quips: "How old would you be if you didn't know how old you were?"; "Age is a question of mind over matter. If you don't mind, it doesn't matter"; and "I've said it once and I'll say it a thousand times: I'm forty-four years old."

What is the Green Monster?

A. Pumpsie Green's nickname
B. slang for the salary envy that eats up baseball players
C. Fenway Park's left-field wall
D. derisive term for AstroTurf
E. Nickname of the 1970's A's dynasty

Answer: C

Extra Bases>

Fenway's 37-foot left-field fence looms just 315 feet from home plate.

THE 1927 YANKEES LINEUP WAS NICKNAMED "_____ ROW."

Answer: Murderer's

Extra Bases>

That lineup featured Babe Ruth, Lou Gehrig, Tony Lazzeri, Earle Combs, and Bob Meusel. Ruth hit 60 homers and had 164 RBIs. Gehrig led the league with 175 RBIs. The Yankees went 110–44, finished 19 games ahead of the A's, and swept the Pirates in the World Series.

MATCH UP OLD-TIME BASEBALL NAMES:

1. Burleigh	A. Cuyler
2. Kiki	B. Shocker
3. Pee Wee	C. Grimes
4. Urban	D. Reese

Answers: 1-C, 2-A, 3-D, 4-B

TRUE OR FALSE:

The famous Boudreau Shift was instituted in an effort to stymie hot-hitting Lou Boudreau.

Answer: False

Extra Bases>

It was instituted *by* Boudreau, player-manager of the Indians, in hopes of slowing down Ted Williams. When the Splendid Splinter, a lefty and notorious pull hitter, came to bat, Boudreau shifted every player except the third baseman and left fielder to the right side of the field.

Q: What is the House That Ruth Built?

A: Yankee Stadium

SLIDERS, CURVES, AND SCREWBALLS ARE ALL EXAMPLES OF A TYPE OF PITCH KNOWN AS A ______ BALL.

Answer: breaking

The movie *A League of Their Own* is about:

A. the Negro Leagues
B. the All American Girls Baseball League, from the 1940s
C. the 1927 Yankees, considered one of the greatest teams ever
D. the St. Louis Browns, one of the worst teams ever
E. a sexy baseball groupie, who builds a field in Iowa, where Jimmy Piersall's ghost shows up, leading to assorted high jinks coupled with several drawn-out tragic deaths, and culminating with a dramatic slow-motion home run that blows up an entire embankment of lights

Answer: B

THE BOSTON BRAVES FAMOUS PENNANT-WINNING FORMULA IN 1948 WAS: "_____ AND _____ AND TWO DAYS OF RAIN."

Answer: Spahn, Sain

Extra Bases>

The saying refers to the fact that the Braves were best off starting their two aces, Warren Spahn (15–12) and Johnny Sain (24–15).

TRUE OR FALSE:

When a pitcher is throwing a no-hitter, it's considered bad luck if teammates mention it to him.

Answer: True

Q: Who signed an autograph that read: "To Johnny Bench, a sure Hall of Famer"?

A: Ted Williams

ON WHAT OCCASION DID LOU GEHRIG ANNOUNCE: ". . . TODAY I CONSIDER MYSELF THE LUCKIEST MAN ON THE FACE OF THE EARTH"?

A. upon breaking into the Yankee's lineup
B. after his first game played side-by-side with Babe Ruth
C. following a Yankees victory in the 1927 World Series
D. after winning the triple crown (.363, 49 HRs, 165 RBIs) in 1934
E. at his farewell speech at Yankees Stadium in 1939

Answer: E

Extra Bases> Gehrig, so strong and durable that he was nicknamed "The Iron Horse," was suffering from a rare disease, amotrophic lateral sclerosis, forever after to be known as "Lou Gehrig's Disease." He died in 1941, just two years after retiring.

A BATTING AVERAGE BELOW .200 IS SAID TO BE BELOW THE ______ LINE.

Answer: Mendoza

Extra Bases>

The term refers to Mario Mendoza, a good-glove/no-hit shortstop who batted below .200 five times during his nine-year career, with the Pirates, Mariners, and Rangers.

True or False:

"Texas Leaguer" is a term for a bloop hit that falls in for a single.

Answer: True

When the Red Sox are playing, fans at Yankee Stadium will often wave placards that read, simply: "1918." What's that all about?

A. It's the year the Red Sox foolishly sold Babe Ruth to the Yankees.
B. It's the year of the Bosox's most recent World Series win.
C. It's the year the Yankees started, ending Boston's dominance of baseball.
D. It's meant to rub in the fact that many Red Sox fans were on the wrong side during World War I.
E. It's Morse Code for "Red Sox stink!"

Answer: B

RECORD BOOK

True or False:

In the post–World War II era, no player has batted .400.

Answer: True

Extra Bases>

Boston's Ted Williams batted .406 in 1941. Since then, a few players have flirted with .400, notably George Brett of the Royals in 1980 (.390), Rod Carew with the Twins in 1977 (.388), and Tony Gwynn, who batted .394 for the Padres during the strike-shortened 1994 season.

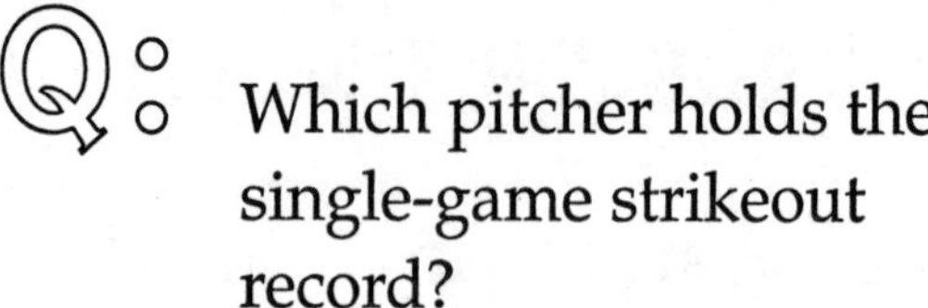

Which pitcher holds the single-game strikeout record?

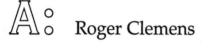

A: Roger Clemens

Extra Bases>

The Red Sox hurler KO'd 20 Mariners in a 1986 contest.

MATCH IMMORTAL NUMBERS WITH THEIR AUTHORS:

1. 755	A. Joe DiMaggio's record consecutive-game hitting streak
2. 61	B. Cy Young's career victory record
3. 56	C. Hank Aaron's career homer record
4. 511	D. Roger Maris's 1961 HR total, a single-season record

Answers: 1-C, 2-D, 3-A, 4-B

IN 1987, A'S FIRST BASEMAN _____ SET A ROOKIE RECORD, HITTING 49 HOMERS.

Answer: Mark McGwire

TRUE OR FALSE:

There has never been a thirty-inning game.

Answer: True

Extra Bases>

On May 1, 1920, Brooklyn's Leon Cadore and Joe Oeschger of the Braves battled to a twenty-six-inning, 1–1 tie.

IN 1988, OREL HERSHISER SET A RECORD BY THROWING HOW MANY CONSECUTIVE SCORELESS INNINGS?

A. 18
B. 44
C. 56
D. 59
E. 98

Answer: D

Q: Who is the only player to have four consecutive four-hit games?

A: Milt Stock (Dodgers third baseman, 1923)

TIGERS ROOKIE RUDY YORK HIT ____ HOMERS IN AUGUST OF 1937, FOR THE MOST PRODUCTIVE MONTH IN BASEBALL HISTORY.

Answer: 18

TRUE OR FALSE:

If walks, errors, and being hit by pitches are taken into account, several players have reached base in more than half of their career plate appearances.

Answer: False

Extra Bases>

But Ted Williams comes close, having reached base 48.3 percent of the time.

ONCE UPON A TIME, THE CAREER RECORD FOR HOMERS WAS A PALTRY 127. WHO OWNED THAT RECORD?

A. Sam Thompson

B. Ty Cobb

C. Nap Lajoie

D. Gil Hodges

E. Chief Bender

Answer: A

Extra Bases> "Big Sam" was a star outfielder for the Phillies in the late nineteenth century. Not too far into the twentieth century, Babe Ruth broke his record, and then some.

Who is the only pitcher to throw a no-hitter as a reliever rather than as a starter?

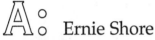

Ernie Shore

Extra Bases> Here's how it happened: Red Sox starter Babe Ruth walked the game's leadoff batter, then got ejected for arguing with the umpire. Shore stepped in. The base runner was shot down trying to steal second. And Shore mowed down the next 26 Senators in a row for a 4–0, no-hit relief effort.

MATCH UP FORMER RECORD HOLDERS WITH THE PLAYERS WHO SURPASSED THEM:

1. Lou Brock (938 stolen bases)
2. Lou Gehrig (2,130 consecutive games)
3. Ty Cobb (4,189 hits)
4. Dave Righetti (46 saves, season)

A. Bobby Thigpen
B. Pete Rose
C. Rickey Henderson
D. Cal Ripken Jr.

Answers: 1-C, 2-D, 3-B, 4-A

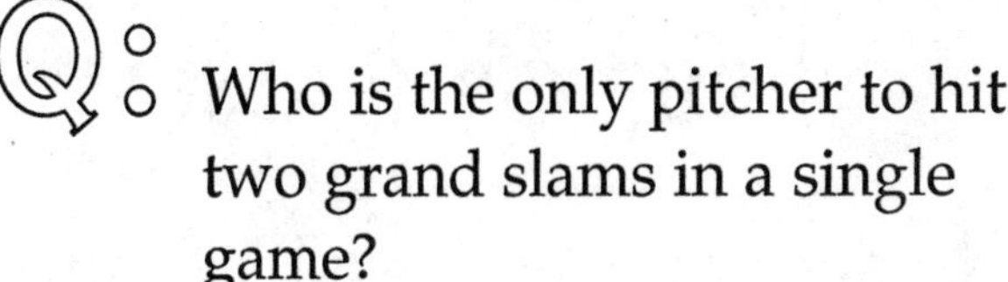

Who is the only pitcher to hit two grand slams in a single game?

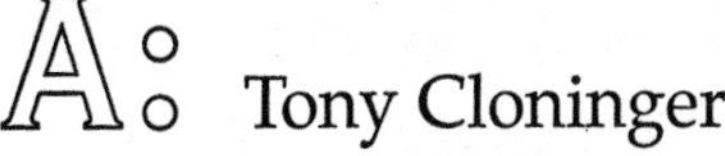

Tony Cloninger

Extra Bases>

Atlanta's Cloninger achieved his feat on July 3, 1966, in a game against the Giants.

TRUE OR FALSE:

No one has ever scored 200 runs in a season.

Answer: True

Extra Bases>

"Sliding" Billy Hamilton came closest, when he scored 196 runs for the Phillies in 1894.

AN 1897 GAME FEATURED THE CUBS BEATING THE LOUISVILLE COLONELS BY THE HIGHEST SCORE EVER:

A. 21–4
B. 27–6
C. 36–7
D. 40–0
E. 41–11

Answer: C

THE GAME-WINNING RBI WAS ONLY KEPT AS AN OFFICIAL STATISTIC FOR TEN YEARS. WHEN IT WAS DROPPED IN 1989, THE ALL-TIME LEADER WAS _____, WITH 129 OF THEM.

Answer: Keith Hernandez

Q: Who is the youngest player ever to reach the 100-homer plateau?

A: Tony Conigliaro

Extra Bases> Conigliaro was touted as the next Ted Williams when he joined the Red Sox in 1964. He reached the century mark at the age of twenty-two. But in 1967, he was hit in the face by a pitch thrown by Jack Hamilton of the Angels. He missed the entire next season and the lingering effects of the beaning—damaged eyesight—led to an early retirement.

True or False:

Among twentieth-century pitchers, there's never been a 40-game winner.

Answer: False

Extra Bases> Jack Chesbro was 41–12 for the New York Highlanders in 1904; Ed Walsh was 40–15 for the White Sox in 1908.

WHAT IS THE INDIVIDUAL RECORD FOR HITS IN A GAME?

A. 5

B. 6

C. 7

D. 9

E. 10

Answer: D

Extra Bases>

On July 10, 1932, Cleveland's Johnny Burnett went 9 for 11 in an eighteen-inning game. He collected seven singles and two doubles, but the A's still won, 18–17.

IN 1930, CUBS OUTFIELDER HACK WILSON SET AN UNAPPROACHABLE RECORD, RACKING UP ______ RBIs.

Answer: 190

Q: Who was the hardest batter to strike out in baseball history?

A: Joe Sewell

Extra Bases>

Sewell was a star shortstop of the '20s who struck out just 114 times in 1,903 games during a career played mostly with the Indians. In 1932, he whiffed just three times in 503 at bats. Overall, Sewell averaged a strikeout every 62.6 at bats, well ahead of his closest competition, Lloyd Waner, who struck out once every 44.9 at bats.

TRUE OR FALSE:

Though Cy Young won 511 games, no other pitcher has ever even broken the 400-victory mark.

Answer: False

Extra Bases>

Walter Johnson was 417–279 during a 21-year career with the Senators, 1907–27.

MATCH UP RECORDS FOR FUTILITY:

1. four straight homers yielded
2. eight errors in a World Series
3. 12 passed balls in a game
4. 189 times KO'd, season

A. Paul Foytack (1963 Angels)
B. Roger Peckinpaugh (1925 Senators)
C. Alexander Gardner (1884 Nationals)
D. Bobby Bonds (1970 Giants)

Answers: 1-A, 2-B, 3-C, 4-D

IN 1986, RED SOX RIGHT FIELDER DWIGHT EVANS MADE HISTORY BY ______ ON THE FIRST ______ OF THE SEASON.

Answer: homering, pitch

What Record Belongs to Johnny Vander Meer?

A. a fastball clocked at 103 mph
B. being the only player to hit a ball clear out of Yankee Stadium
C. hurling back-to-back no-hitters
D. his .428 mark in 1924, highest single-season batting average ever
E. overcoming extreme prejudice to become baseball's first Dutchman

Answer: C

Extra Bases> In 1938, while pitching for the Reds, Vander Meer no-hit the Boston Bees, 3–0, on June 11, and in his next start, on June 15, no-hit the Dodgers, 6–0. Incredibly, in the start that followed, Vander Meer flirted with three in a row, taking a no-hitter into the fourth inning.

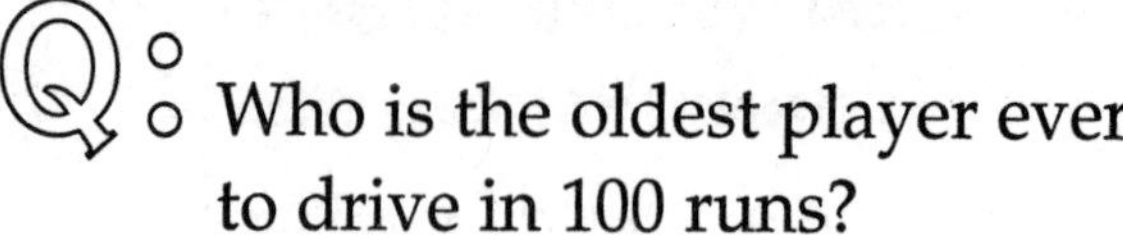

Q: Who is the oldest player ever to drive in 100 runs?

A: Dave Winfield

Extra Bases>

During Toronto's 1992 championship season, the forty-two-year-old slugger batted .290 with 26 homers and 108 RBIs.

ON SEPTEMBER 7, 1993, ______ HAD A PHENOMENALLY PRODUCTIVE GAME, GOING 4 FOR 5 WITH FOUR HOMERS AND 12 RBIS, A TOTAL MATCHED ONLY ONE OTHER TIME IN BASEBALL HISTORY.

Answer: Mark Whiten (Cardinals outfielder)

True or False:

No pitcher has ever won 20 games in a row during a season.

Answer: True

Extra Bases>

Rube Marquard won 19 straight for the Giants in 1912.

THE RECORD FOR HITS IN A SEASON BELONGS TO:

A. Ty Cobb
B. George Sisler
C. Ted Williams
D. Wade Boggs
E. Tony Gwynn

Answer: B

Extra Bases>

The St. Louis Browns first baseman racked up 257 hits in 1920, a number since unapproached.

Q: What pitcher holds the all-time record for strikeouts?

A: Nolan Ryan

Extra Bases>

Ryan racked up 5,714 strikeouts over 27 seasons played with the Mets, Angels, Astros, and Rangers.

TRUE OR FALSE:

Orioles defensive whiz Brooks Robinson earned six Gold Gloves, a record among third basemen.

Answer: False

Extra Bases>

Try 16 . . . in a row! (1960 to 1975).

ON APRIL 21, 1898, FROSTY BILL DUGGLEBY OF THE PHILLIES BECAME THE FIRST AND ONLY PLAYER TO HIT A ______ IN HIS INITIAL BIG-LEAGUE AT BAT.

Answer: grand slam

Extra Bases>
What's more, Duggleby was a pitcher.

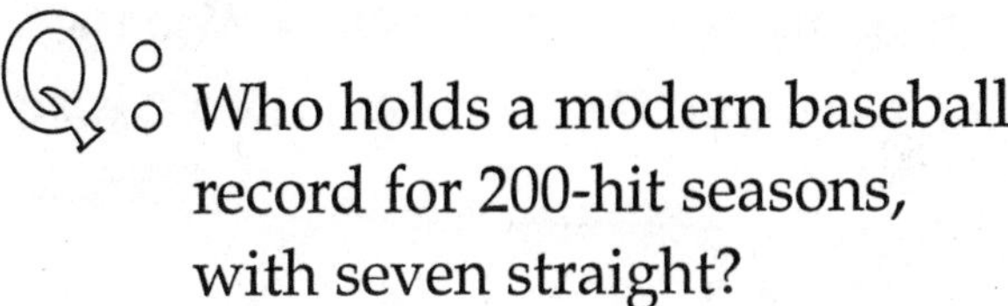

Q: Who holds a modern baseball record for 200-hit seasons, with seven straight?

A: Wade Boggs

Extra Bases>

Boggs racked up 200-plus hits 1983–89, while playing third base for the Red Sox.

What do Dale Long, Don Mattingly, and Ken Griffey Jr. have in common?

A. They're all Yankees stars.
B. They're the top three, career grand-slam list.
C. They share a record, hitting homers in eight straight games.
D. They are the only twentieth-century players to have 150 RBI seasons.
E. They are the only three players pre-approved for the Hall of Fame.

Answer: C

TRUE OR FALSE:

Willie McCovey holds the record for intentional walks in a season.

Answer: True

Extra Bases>

The fearsome Giants first baseman received 45 of them in 1970, a year in which he hit 39 homers and drove in 126 runs.

In his spectacular 1968 season, ______ posted a 1.12 ERA, breaking Walter Johnson's 55-year-old record for lowest ERA, 300-plus innings pitched.

Answer: Bob Gibson (Cardinals)

MATCH UP PITCHING RECORDS:

1. ten strikeouts in a row
2. no-hitters first two seasons
3. won both ends of a doubleheader
4. nine career ERA titles

A. Joe McGinnity
B. Tom Seaver
C. Lefty Grove
D. Steve Busby

Answers: 1-B, 2-D, 3-A, 4-C

THE RECORD FOR SHUTOUTS IN A SEASON BELONGS TO:

A. Jim Kaat
B. Mickey Lolich
C. Don Sutton
D. Grover Cleveland Alexander
E. Dean Chance

Answer: D (16 for the Phillies in 1916)

In 1968, Frank Howard, a 6′8″, 275-lb. Senators slugger, went on a rampage, hitting ______ homers in 20 at bats over a six-game span.

Answer: ten

TRUE OR FALSE:

Hank Aaron holds the world record for career homers.

Answer: False

Extra Bases>

The honor belongs to Sadaharu Oh, a star for Japan's Yomiuri Giants, who hit 868 homers during his career.

RULE BOOK

On April 10, 1976, with the bases loaded, bottom of the ninth, Milwaukee trailing the Yankees, 9–6, Don Money stepped to the plate and hit what appeared to be a game-winning grand slam. But it was disallowed because:

A. time had been called
B. Money was not in proper uniform
C. it actually hooked foul
D. Money passed another runner on the base paths
E. a fan interfered with Yankee outfielder Roy White as he tried to make the catch

Answer: A

Extra Bases> Forced to try, try again, Money hit a sacrifice fly and the Brewers lost 9–7.

A FAIR BALL POP-UP, WITH RUNNERS ON FIRST AND SECOND, OR WITH THE BASES LOADED AND LESS THAN TWO OUTS, IS KNOWN AS AN ______ AND THE BATTER IS AUTOMATICALLY RULED OUT. THIS IS TO PREVENT A SLY INFIELDER FROM INTENTIONALLY LETTING THE BALL HIT THE GROUND AND THEN TRYING TO TURN A DOUBLE PLAY.

Answer: infield fly

TRUE OR FALSE:

A runner rounds first base, makes a preliminary move toward second, then heads back toward first and is tagged before he reaches the base. He should not be called out because players are allowed to overrun first base.

Answer: False

Extra Bases> Players are allowed to overrun first base, but they must not make even a hint of a move toward second base in the process. If a player does, he's fair game.

WHAT IS THE PROPER CALL IN EACH OF THESE SITUATIONS INVOLVING PITCHERS?

1. pitcher throws while time is called
2. pitcher deliberately throws a beanball
3. pitcher caught throwing a spitball (first offense)
4. pitcher fakes a delivery to home plate

A. ball
B. balk
C. no pitch
D. ejection

Answers: 1-C, 2-D, 3-A, 4-B

Extra Bases> The first time a pitcher gets caught throwing a spitball, the pitch is called a ball, the pitcher gets a warning, and the rules call for an announcer to explain what's happening over the public address system. If the pitcher is caught a second time, he's kicked out of the game.

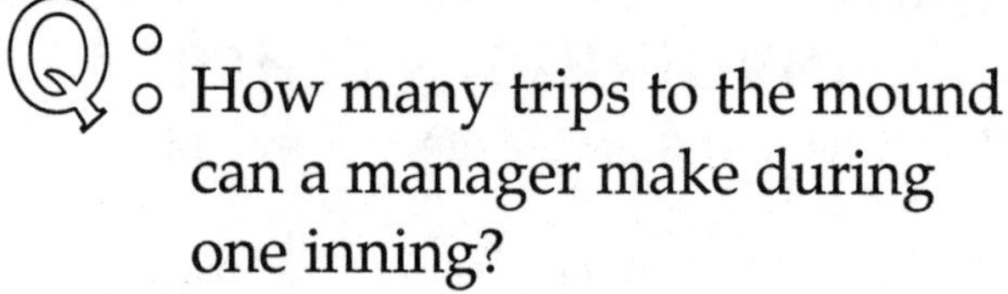

Q: How many trips to the mound can a manager make during one inning?

A: one

Extra Bases>

Another visit automatically necessitates the pitcher's removal.

During a 1992 contest, when Expos outfielder Larry Walker hit a fly ball that struck a speaker suspended from the roof of Olympic Stadium, why was it called a homer?

A. Judging from the trajectory of the ball, it would have been a homer.

B. It's the call according to that particular stadium's ground rules.

C. Hitting a speaker always goes for a homer.

D. It's just plain impressive to strike something that's 150 feet in the air.

E. Canadian rules require it.

Answer: B

TRUE OR FALSE:

In the early days of the American League, a batter could call his own pitches—"fastball," "slowball," "curveball"—just like in kickball.

Answer: False

Extra Bases> But the National Association did initially allow batters to request pitches that were either high or low.

IF A PLAYER COLLECTS A SINGLE, DOUBLE, TRIPLE, AND HOMER IN THE SAME GAME, IT'S KNOWN AS HITTING FOR THE _____ .

Answer: cycle

Q: How many warm-up tosses are pitchers allowed, both upon entering the game and between innings?

A: eight

OVER THE COURSE OF BASEBALL HISTORY, WHICH OF THE FOLLOWING EQUALED A WALK?

A. four balls
B. five balls
C. seven balls
D. eight balls
E. all of the above

Answer: E

Extra Bases>

It's been as high as nine, and in baseball's very earliest years walks simply didn't exist.

True or False:

Metal bats are illegal in the big leagues.

Answer: True

What would a pitcher's ERA be if in his initial appearance of the season he gave up some runs, then left the game before recording any outs?

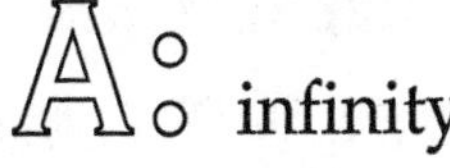

infinity

Extra Bases>

Yankees reliever Steve Howe walked away from a disastrous first outing of the 1993 season with an infinite ERA.

A GROUND BALL IS HIT TO A SECOND BASEMAN, WHO IN TURN THROWS THE BALL TO FIRST IN TIME TO GET THE RUNNER. CREDIT THE SECOND BASEMAN WITH AN

________ .

Answer: assist

MATCH UP NUMBER OF RUNS THAT RESULT FROM EACH OF THESE SITUATIONS:

1. ground rule double with bases loaded	A. 0
2 balk with runner on third	B. 1
3. team wins by forfeit	C. 2
4. runner crosses plate before force at first ends inning	D. 9

Answers: 1-C, 2-B, 3-D, 4-A

TRUE OR FALSE:

If a runner tags up and advances on a fly ball that's caught, it's deemed a sacrifice fly and the batter is not assessed an at bat.

Answer: False

Extra Bases>

Only when the runner scores from third. Otherwise, it's just a plain old flyout, and counts as an at bat.

THE DISTANCE BETWEEN THE BASES IS ______ FEET.

Answer: 90

Q: If a pitcher is responsible for a pitch that gets past the catcher, it's scored a "wild pitch." But if it's judged to be the catcher's fault, what is it scored as?

A: passed ball

TRUE OR FALSE:

In baseball's early days, home plate was square.

Answer: True

Extra Bases>

In 1900, the NL changed the shape from a square to a pentagon. It was hoped that this would end arguments with umpires over strike calls.

IN 1977, BRAVES OWNER ______ TOOK OVER AS MANAGER IN AN EFFORT TO HALT A 16-GAME LOSING STREAK. HIS TENURE LASTED JUST ONE GAME—ANOTHER LOSS—BEFORE HE WAS RELIEVED OF HIS DUTIES DUE TO RULES STATING THAT AN OWNER CANNOT ALSO ACT AS MANAGER.

Answer: Ted Turner

True or False:

If a player steps out of the batter's box while making contact with a pitch, he is automatically out.

Answer: True

Extra Bases>

Hank Aaron hit a homer in 1965 that quickly turned to an out when the ump noticed he'd stepped out of the box during his swing.

Q: What is the call if an umpire spreads out his arms, palms turned down?

A: safe

On July 26, 1935, Jesse Hill of the Yankees hit a liner that ricocheted off pitcher Ed Linke's head. Jack Redmond, the Senators catcher, caught the ball on the rebound and threw to second to nab Ben Chapman who'd strayed off the bag. Score that a _____-_____-_____ double play.

Answer: 1-2-4

In a 1931 contest, Lou Gehrig hit an apparent homer. But his Yankees teammate Lyn Lary rounded third base, then headed straight for the dugout. Gehrig went ahead and circled the bases until the umpires made what call?

A. Lary scored, but Gehrig was called out for passing him on the base paths.

B. Gehrig was credited with a solo homer only.

C. Lary was called out for leaving the field; Gehrig was also called out for passing Lary on the base paths, and his homer was reduced to a triple.

D. Gehrig was called out and Lary was sent back to third.

E. Lary was called out; Gehrig had to stop at second.

Answer: C

Extra Bases> The end of the season found Gehrig and Ruth tied for the league lead, with 46 homers apiece. Thus, Lary's gaffe cost Gehrig sole possession of the AL home-run title.

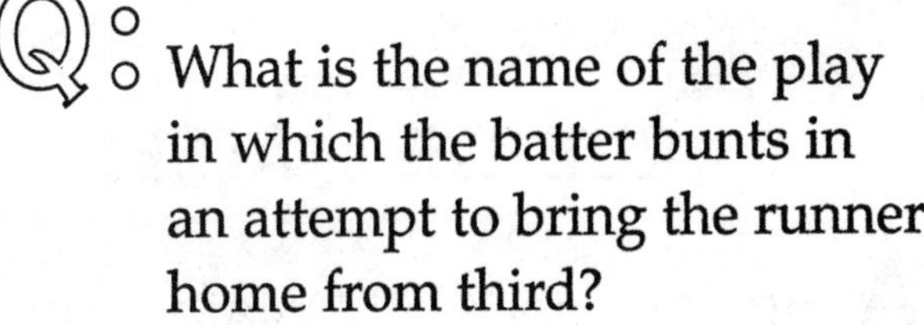

Q: What is the name of the play in which the batter bunts in an attempt to bring the runner home from third?

A: squeeze play

TRUE OR FALSE:

A player needs 502 plate appearances to qualify for the batting title.

Answer: True

IN 1893, THE PITCHER'S MOUND WAS MOVED BACK FROM 50 FEET AWAY FROM HOMEPLATE TO ITS CURRENT DISTANCE, ______.

Answer: 60'6"

Extra Bases>

Some say the mound was moved back to give hitters more of a chance against Giants ace Amos Rusie. "The Hoosier Thunderbolt" had led the league in strikeouts three of his first five seasons, twice with totals above 300.

MATCH ILL-CONSIDERED ACTS WITH PLAYERS WHO MADE RAPID EXITS:

1. spit in an umpire's face	A. Heinie Manush
2. slugged an umpire	B. Bret Saberhagen
3. snapped an ump's bowtie	C. Frenchy Bordagaray
4. sang "Three Blind Mice" to an ump	D. Pink Hawley

Answers: 1-C, 2-D, 3-A, 4-B

Extra Bases>

Reds pitcher Hawley punched an umpire in 1897, when the game was more rough-and-tumble. Bordagaray, a Dodgers star in the '30s, was fined $500 for the spitting incident, leading to his famous quip: "The penalty is a little more than I expectorated."

TRUE OR FALSE:

There is no set rule regulating the minimum distance a fence must be situated from home plate.

Answer: False

Extra Bases>

The official minimum is 250 feet, and parks are urged to allow at least 320 feet down the lines and 400 to straight-away center.

Boston's Howard Ehmke threw a September 7, 1923, no-hitter against the A's that was preserved thanks to:

A. rain erasing an inning in which two batters reached safely
B. an opposing hitter failing to touch first base on a double
C. the official scorer changing a hit to an error
D. a hit by a player who turned out to be batting out of order
E. a lucky rabbit's foot, repeating the word "terrapin" before each pitch, and wearing a left sock that hadn't been washed all season

Answer: B

Q: While one batter stands at the plate, where does the batter who's next in line wait?

A: on deck circle

TEAMS MUST PLAY ______ FULL INNINGS FOR A GAME TO BE DEEMED OFFICIAL.

Answer: five

TRUE OR FALSE:

Spitballs were once legal.

Answer: True

Extra Bases>

They were outlawed in 1920, but with a grandfather clause to accommodate hurlers who depended on the spitter as their, er, bread-and-butter pitch. Among the exempted: Stan Coveleski, Bill Doak, Red Faber, and Burleigh Grimes.

IN THE COURSE OF 550 PLATE APPEARANCES DURING A SEASON, JOHNNY HYPOTHETICAL GETS 150 HITS, REACHES BASE ON ERRORS 12 TIMES, WALKS 40 TIMES AND IS HIT BY 10 PITCHES. HIS BATTING AVERAGE IS _____.

Answer: .300

Extra Bases>

To arrive at Johnny's average, take 550 plate appearances and subtract his walks and hit-by-pitches to come up with his number of at bats: 500. (Note: if Johnny reaches base on error, it still counts as an at bat.) Divide 150 hits by 500 at bats to come up with Mr. Hypothetical's batting average.

Why haven't the Tigers retired Ty Cobb's number?

A. Why celebrate such a despised ballplayer?

B. Number 5 is too popular with too many players.

C. He wore a wide variety of numbers during his playing career.

D. He wore no number during his playing career.

E. There are no records indicating what number he wore, and strangely, no photos of him with his back turned.

Answer: D

Extra Bases>

The American League didn't make uniform numbers mandatory until 1931.

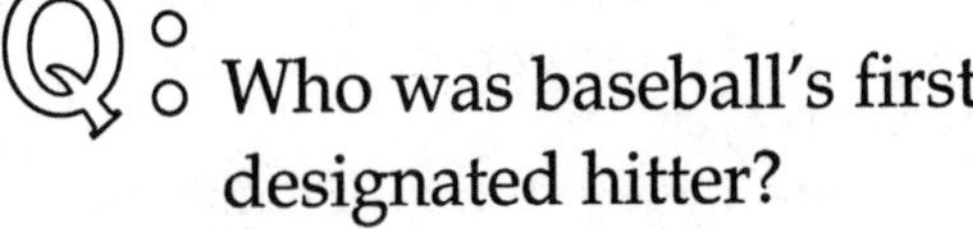

Who was baseball's first designated hitter?

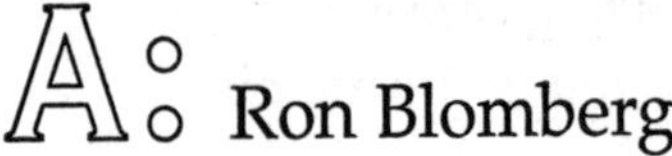

Ron Blomberg

Extra Bases>

The DH rule was adopted in the AL for the start of the '73 season and Blomberg of the Yankees was the very first to bat in this new capacity.

WHAT IS THE PROPER CALL IN EACH OF THESE SITUATIONS INVOLVING BATTERS?

1. batter hits ball, fielder throws his glove and deflects it
2. batter swings at pitch that then hits him
3. batter makes contact with ball twice on one swing
4. batter swings and makes contact with catcher's mitt

A. strike

B. out

C. single

D. triple

Answers: 1-D, 2-A, 3-B, 4-C

OFFICIALLY, THE STRIKE ZONE EXTENDS FROM THE TOP OF A BATTER'S ________ TO THE TOP OF HIS ________.

Answer: shoulders, knees

True or False:

In 1993, when a fly ball hit Rangers outfielder Jose Canseco in the head and bounced over the fence, it was ruled a ground rule double.

Answer: False

Extra Bases>

It was a homer. If it had touched the ground and bounced over the fence, then it would have been a ground rule double.

Bloopers, Bad Hops, and General Buffoonery

In one of baseball's most memorable miscues, ______ allowed a Mookie Wilson grounder to roll between his legs, setting the stage for the Mets to rally past the Red Sox in the 1986 World Series.

Answer: Bill Buckner (first baseman)

RANGERS PITCHER GREG HARRIS MISSED TWO STARTS IN 1987 DUE TO INJURIES SUFFERED WHILE:

A. brushing his teeth
B. flicking sunflower seeds
C. walking a dog
D. tying his shoes
E. sleeping

Answer: B

True or False:

The Astrodome's original playing field featured natural grass.

Answer: True

Extra Bases>

But grass didn't grow greener inside the Dome. Tifway 419 Bermuda, a type of grass specifically chosen for the great indoors, died and was replaced by AstroTurf.

Match Up Brawl-Mates:

1. Juan Marichal
2. Pete Rose
3. Billy Martin
4. Rob Dibble

A. slid into, then fought, Mets second baseman Bud Harrelson

B. plunked Tim Teufel, who then rushed the mound

C. skulled L.A. catcher John Roseboro with a bat

D. broke the cheekbone of Cubs rookie Jim Brewer

Answers: 1-C, 2-A, 3-D, 4-B

Q: What dictator of a small island nation was also once a hot prospect among big-league scouts?

A: Fidel Castro

Extra Bases>

Castro had a great curveball and turned down a $5,000 signing bonus from the Giants, choosing instead to go to law school, wage guerrilla warfare, assume power, grow a thick beard, smoke cigars, and rule Cuba with an iron hand.

MEATLOAF'S HIT "PARADISE BY THE DASHBOARD LIGHT" WINDS UP WITH A DOUBLE-ENTENDRE-LADEN "PLAY-BY-PLAY," COURTESY OF LONG-TIME YANKEE ANNOUNCER ______.

Answer: Phil "Scooter" Rizzuto

What was unusual about the fan who retrieved Royals star George Brett's 300th career homer, hit at Cleveland Stadium in 1993?

A. It was a man from Madagascar, attending his first baseball game.
B. It was his brother Ken, himself a former big leaguer.
C. It was an 11-month-old baby girl.
D. It was a blind man.
E. It was Siamese twins.

Answer: D

TRUE OR FALSE:

A's owner Charlie O. Finley deemed June 18, 1972, "Mustache Day," with a promise of a $300 bonus to any one of his players who grew one.

Answer: True

Extra Bases>

Every member of his team collected the bonus, among them Catfish Hunter, Rollie Fingers, Joe Rudi, and Gene Tenace.

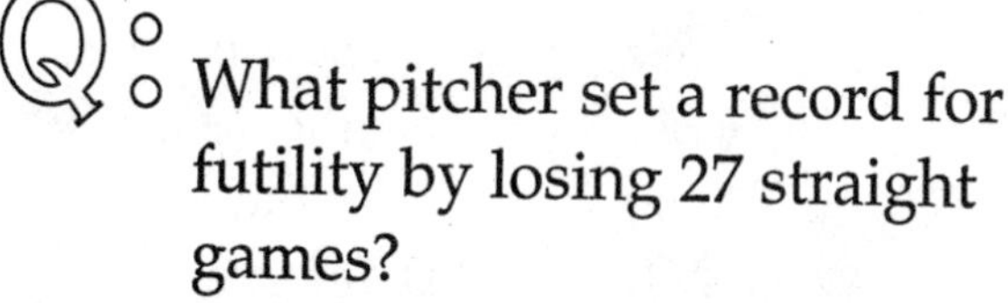

Q: What pitcher set a record for futility by losing 27 straight games?

A: Anthony Young (Mets)

MATCH BALLPLAYERS WITH CRIMINAL ACTS:

1. Sam Crane
2. Denny McLain
3. Luis Polonia
4. Willie Wilson

A. racketeering
B. drug use
C. statutory rape
D. murder

Answers: 1-D, 2-A, 3-C, 4-B

Extra Bases>

Crane was a light-hitting journeyman shortstop, who spent time in the big leagues from 1914 to 1922 and time in the penitentiary afterward, for killing his girlfriend and her male companion.

In 1973, Yankee pitchers Fritz Peterson and Mike Kekich got caught up in the Swinging '70s and generated what tabloid scandal?

A. They were baseball's first openly homosexual couple.

B. The two got busted for quaaludes at Studio 54.

C. Both pitchers insisted on wearing leisure suits to team events.

D. They traded families—as in literally swapped wives, kids, even pets.

E. They engaged in a locker-room fistfight over Donna Summer concert tickets.

Answer: D

FOR A 1993 GAME, THE BREWERS HAD GRAEME LLOYD ON THE MOUND AND DAVE NILSSON BEHIND THE PLATE, MARKING THE FIRST TIME A TEAM HAS EVER FIELDED A BATTERY HAILING FROM ______.

Answer: Australia

Q: Among pitchers, who is the only 200-game loser who is not also a 200-game winner?

A: Bob Friend

Extra Bases>

Friend was 197–230 over a 16-year career, played mostly with the Pirates.

BO BELINSKY, ONE-TIME ANGELS PITCHER AND PLAYBOY PAR EXCELLENCE, WAS ROMANTICALLY LINKED WITH ALL BUT ONE OF THE FOLLOWING WOMEN:

A. Ann-Margret
B. Tina Louise
C. Mamie Van Doren
D. Kim Novak
E. Connie Stevens

Answer: D

TRUE OR FALSE:

The first uniforms consisted of blue wool pants, white flannel shirts, and straw hats.

Answer: True

Extra Bases>

The New York Knickerbockers sported them for the 1849 season.

ZACK TAYLOR, MANAGER OF THE HAPLESS ST. LOUIS BROWNS, USED ______ DIFFERENT PITCHERS IN A NINE-INNING, 4–3 LOSS TO THE WHITE SOX IN 1949.

Answer: nine

Q: Off of whom did pitcher Joe Niekro hit the only homer of his 22-year career?

A: Phil Niekro (his brother)

AMONG PLAYERS WITH 20-HOMER SEASONS, KEVIN MAAS MANAGED THE LOWEST RBI TOTAL EVER. FOR THE YANKEES IN 1990, MAAS HIT 21 HOMERS AND DROVE IN HOW MANY RUNS?

A. 21
B. 30
C. 41
D. 52
E. 78

Answer: C

TRUE OR FALSE:

Carlos May's birth date was conspicuously displayed on his uniform.

Answer: True

Extra Bases>

May, who played from 1968 to 1977 for the White Sox, Yankees, and Angels, had May 17 for a birth date. Sly Carlos chose 17 as his jersey number. Thus, his uniform read "May 17."

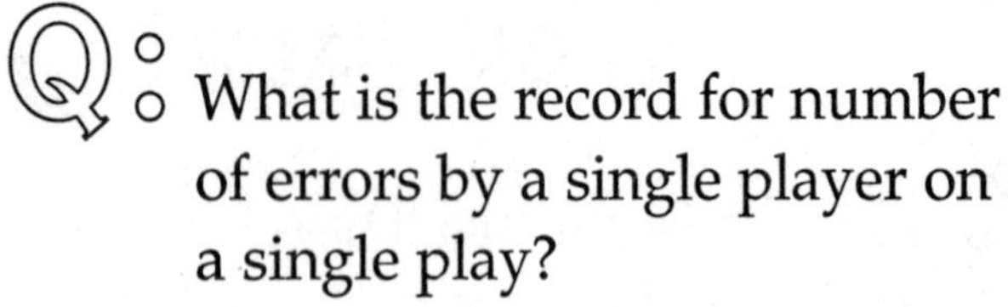

Q: What is the record for number of errors by a single player on a single play?

A: three

Extra Bases>

Yankees hurler Tommy John was the culprit during a 1988, 16–3, blowout of the Brewers.

In a famous event, hard-luck fan Charley Lupica climbed atop a flagpole, swearing he wouldn't come down until the ______ moved into first place. He gave up after 117 days, with his team now in fourth place. They finished up the 1949 season in third.

Answer: Indians

MATCH ERRATIC ACTS WITH PLAYERS WHO DID 'EM:

1. ran bases backwards to celebrate 100th homer
2. claims to have pitched no-hitter on acid
3. urinated on each and every big-league field
4. pulled down pants, sat on cake replica of Fenway Park, making quite an impression

A. Rick Bosetti

B. Sparky Lyle

C. Jimmy Piersall

D. Dock Ellis

Answers: 1-C, 2-D, 3-A, 4-B

WHO HOLDS THE RECORD FOR HITTING INTO THE MOST DOUBLE PLAYS IN A SEASON?

A. Willie Horton
B. Andres Galarraga
C. Juan Gonzalez
D. Jim Rice
E. Jackie Jensen

Answer: D (36 with the Red Sox in 1984)

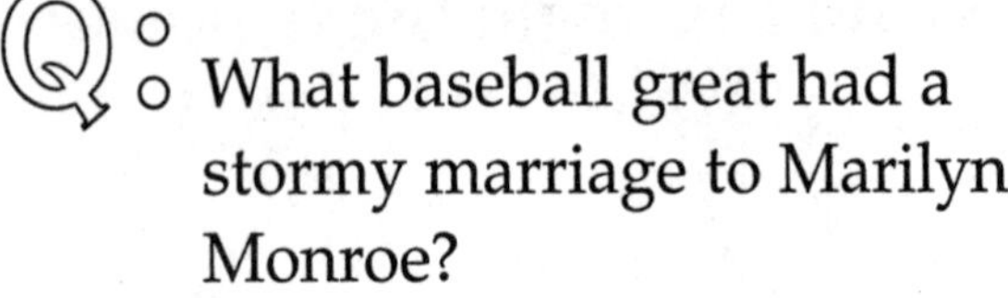

Q: What baseball great had a stormy marriage to Marilyn Monroe?

A: Joe DiMaggio

Reds outfielder Cesar Geronimo had a knack for being in the wrong place at the wrong time: he was strikeout victim number _____ for both Bob Gibson and Nolan Ryan.

Answer: 3,000

TRUE OR FALSE:

A's catcher Ossee Schreckengost had a clause written into the contract of his roommate, Rube Waddell, stating that the Hall of Fame hurler could not eat crackers in bed.

Answer: True

WHAT NOTORIOUSLY LIGHT HITTER DIDN'T RECORD HIS FIRST HOMER UNTIL AT BAT NUMBER 1,381?

A. Freddie Patek
B. Duane Kuiper
C. Rey Sanchez
D. Walt Weiss
E. Kevin Mitchell

Answer: B

Extra Bases>

The Indians second baseman finally connected in 1977. In 1,997 subsequent at bats he failed to hit another.

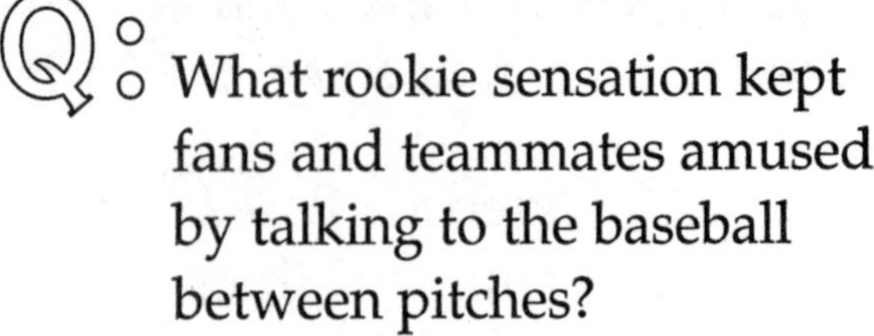

Q: What rookie sensation kept fans and teammates amused by talking to the baseball between pitches?

A: Mark "The Bird" Fidrych

Extra Bases>

Fidrych went 19–9 for the Tigers in 1976. But arm trouble short-circuited his promising career.

TRUE OR FALSE:

A teenage girl once struck out Ruth and Gehrig.

Answer: True

Extra Bases> Sort of. During a 1931 exhibition game, the Chattanooga Lookouts of the Southern Association sent seventeen-year-old Jackie Mitchell to the mound. She proceeded to KO the two Yankee greats. But accounts of the game suggest the strikeouts owed more to chivalry than to any special pitching acumen on the part of Mitchell. Ruth swung wildly twice and took a called third strike. Gehrig, always the gentleman, is said to have intentionally mistimed his swings.

AS A PUBLICITY STUNT, ENGINEERED BY KANSAS CITY A'S OWNER CHARLIE O. FINLEY, BERT CAMPANERIS PLAYED _____ DIFFERENT POSITIONS IN A GAME AGAINST THE ANGELS, ON SEPTEMBER 8, 1965.

Answer: nine

EDD ROUSH, A STAR CENTER FIELDER FOR THE REDS, WAS THROWN OUT OF A 1920 GAME FOR:

A. saying "dammit" within earshot of fans
B. kicking dirt on an umpire
C. playing his position in an advanced state of intoxication
D. falling asleep in the outfield
E. picking dandelions

Answer: D

TRUE OR FALSE:

Reggie "Mr. October" Jackson was "Mr. Strikeout" much of the rest of the time, and set a career record for futility with 2,597 KOs.

Answer: True

BASEBALL AND BIRDS HAVE CROSSED PATHS REPEATEDLY OVER THE YEARS. MATCH UP "FOWL" PLAYS:

1. killed a seagull with a warm-up toss
2. hit a fly ball that struck a dove, fell for a single
3. doffed his cap, releasing a captured sparrow
4. while on the mound, a seagull crapped on him

A. Dion James
B. Ellis Kinder
C. Dave Winfield
D. Casey Stengel

Answers: 1-C, 2-A, 3-D, 4-B

In 1989, _____ was suspended from baseball for gambling by Commissioner A. Bartlett Giamatti.

Answer: Pete Rose

Q: Who is the only player in modern baseball history to die as a result of being hit by a pitch?

A: Ray Chapman

Extra Bases>

On August 16, 1920, the Indians shortstop was hit in the head by a pitch thrown by Carl Mays of the Yankees. He was rushed to the hospital, but never regained consciousness, and died 12 hours later.

When John Kennedy became the Senators catcher in 1962, what similarities did he share with the man who was President of the United States at the time?

A. the same name
B. a home in Washington
C. the same birth date, May 29
D. all of the above
E. a fling with actress Judith Exner

Answer: D

MATCH MISMATCHED TRADES:

1. Red Sox trade Sparky Lyle to
2. Cubs trade Lou Brock to
3. Mets trade Nolan Ryan to
4. Cardinals trade Steve Carlton to

A. Cardinals for Ernie Broglio
B. Phillies for Rick Wise
C. Yankees for Danny Cater
D. Angels for Jim Fregosi

Answers: 1-C, 2-A, 3-D, 4-B

TRUE OR FALSE:

The Astrodome has never had a rainout.

Answer: False

Extra Bases>

- A June 15, 1976, contest had to be postponed because heavy rains made it difficult for players and fans to get to the ballpark.

Q: Who posted the worst average of all time for a full-time player?

A: Rob Deer

Extra Bases>

In 1991, the Tigers right fielder batted .179 with 25 homers and 64 RBIs.

All but one of the following are Yogi-isms (examples of the wit and wisdom of Yankee Hall of Fame catcher Lawrence Peter "Yogi" Berra):

A. "It ain't over 'til it's over."
B. "We made too many wrong mistakes."
C. "Baseball is 90 percent mental. The other half is physical."
D. "Never assume. You will make an 'ass' out of 'you' and 'me.'"
E. "A nickel ain't worth a dime anymore."

Answer: D

True or False:

A big-league team once sent a midget to bat.

Answer: True

Extra Bases> Bill Veeck, owner of the sorry St. Louis Browns, engineered a stunt in which 3′ 7″ Eddie Gaedel jumped out of a cake before the second game of an August 18, 1951, doubleheader with the Tigers. Gaedel came to bat in the nightcap, clutching a tiny bat and wearing uniform number "1/8." He walked on four pitches. A furious AL president put the kibosh on any further shenanigans Veeck might have planned for Gaedel.

BOTTOM OF THE NINTH

TRUE OR FALSE:

Fred Goldsmith is generally considered to be the "inventor" of the curveball.

Answer: False

Extra Bases> Credit usually goes to Candy Cummings, who claimed to have invented the curveball as a teenager. Cummings pitched for several professional teams in the 1870s and later wrote an article entitled "How I Pitched the First Curve." Goldsmith, meanwhile, held the first public demonstration of a curveball in 1870. Still, he's not generally credited with being the curveball's inventor. Goldsmith died, apparently a bitter man, in 1939, the same year Cummings was inducted into the Hall of Fame.

The save became an official statistic in 1969. Dodgers hurler ______ was credited with the first one when he stepped in to preserve a 3–2 win over the Reds.

Answer: Bill Singer

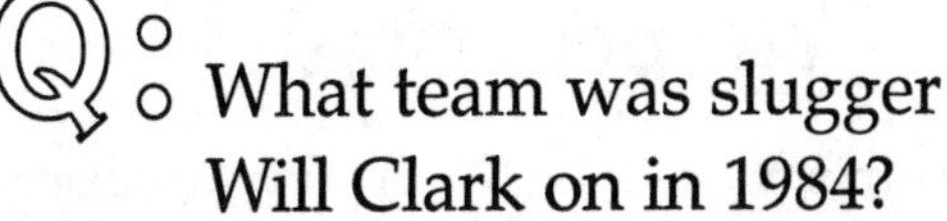

Q: What team was slugger Will Clark on in 1984?

A: the U.S. Olympic baseball team

MATCH UP FAMOUS HOMERS AND THE PITCHERS WHO YIELDED THEM:

1. Babe Ruth's 60th in 1927
2. Roger Maris's 61st in 1961
3. Hank Aaron's career 714th in 1974
4. Hank Aaron's career 715th in 1975

A. Tracy Stallard

B. Al Downing

C. Jack Billingham

D. Tom Zachary

Answers: 1-D, 2-A, 3-C, 4-B

Why is it ironic that a Shoeless Joe Jackson signature fetched $23,100 at a 1990 auction, the most ever for a nineteenth- or twentieth-century John Hancock?

A. Shoeless Joe was convicted for rigging a World Series.
B. Shoeless Joe never made more than $3,000 a year as a player.
C. That's how much the "Black Sox" were paid to throw the 1919 Series.
D. Shoeless Joe was illiterate.
E. The signature was clearly a forgery.

Answer: D

Extra Bases> Shoeless Joe's wife wrote his signature on a piece of paper, and he would meticulously copy it when it was necessary for him to sign his name. In a famous incident, Jackson hit a triple and was subsequently heckled by a Cleveland fan who demanded to know if he could spell "illiterate." Fed up, Jackson shot back: "Hey, big mouth, how do you spell triple?"

True or False:

No 20-game winner has ever had an ERA above 5.00.

Answer: False

Extra Bases>

Bobo Newsom went 20–16 with a 5.08 ERA for the 1938 St. Louis Browns.

THE FACT THAT CASEY CANDAELE'S ______ PLAYED PRO BALL MAKES THE UTILITY MAN FOR THE ASTROS AND EXPOS A BASEBALL LEGACY.

Answer: mother

Extra Bases>

Helen Callahan St. Aubin, plain "Mom" to Casey, played in the All American Girls Baseball League from 1942 to 1954.

Q: Who is the only player to collect hits for two different big-league teams during a single day?

A: Joel Youngblood

Extra Bases>

On August 4, 1982, Youngblood collected a hit for the Mets during an afternoon game at Wrigley. Then he was traded to the Expos, joined them in Philadelphia in time for their night game, and picked up another hit.

MATCH UP THE NAMES OF NEGRO LEAGUE TEAMS:

1. Birmingham
2. Homestead
3. Kansas City
4. Indianapolis

A. Black Barons
B. Clowns
C. Grays
D. Monarchs

Answers: 1-A, 2-C, 3-D, 4-B

WHAT INDIANS ROOKIE SENSATION IMPRESSED TEAMMATES BY OPENING BEER BOTTLES WITH HIS EYE SOCKETS?

A. Eddie Murray
B. Kenny Lofton
C. Joe Charboneau
D. Albert Belle
E. Charles Nagy

Answer: C

Extra Bases>

Charboneau was the AL Rookie of the Year in 1980, when he batted .289 with 23 HRs and 87 RBIs.

TRUE OR FALSE:

Twins star Tony Oliva is the only player ever to win batting titles in his first two seasons.

Answer: True

BETWEEN HIS PLAYING DAYS WITH THE YANKEES AND BECOMING PRESIDENT OF THE AMERICAN LEAGUE, BOBBY BROWN HAD A SUCCESSFUL CAREER AS A _____.

Answer: surgeon

Q: Who are the only two players to hit five homers in a double-header?

A: Nate Colbert and Stan Musial

Extra Bases> Colbert did it for the Padres in 1972, Musial for the Cardinals in 1954. As an odd twist, an eight-year-old Colbert was in the stands at Sportsman's Park for Musial's big day.

WHAT IS THE NAME OF PITCHER JACK MCDOWELL'S ALTERNATIVE ROCK BAND?

A. Blackjack
B. Hurl
C. Pere Ubu
D. V.I.E.W.
E. The Scrimshaw Nosepickers

Answer: D

Extra Bases>
The band once opened for the Smithereens.

TRUE OR FALSE:

Hank Aaron and Babe Ruth are both Aquarians.

Answer: True

Extra Bases>

Aaron was born February 5, 1934, and Ruth on February 6, 1895. The two were fated by the stars to hit a total of 1,469 homers.

ON OPENING DAY 1910, _____ BECAME THE FIRST U.S. PRESIDENT TO THROW OUT THE FIRST PITCH IN A BALL GAME.

Answer: William Howard Taft

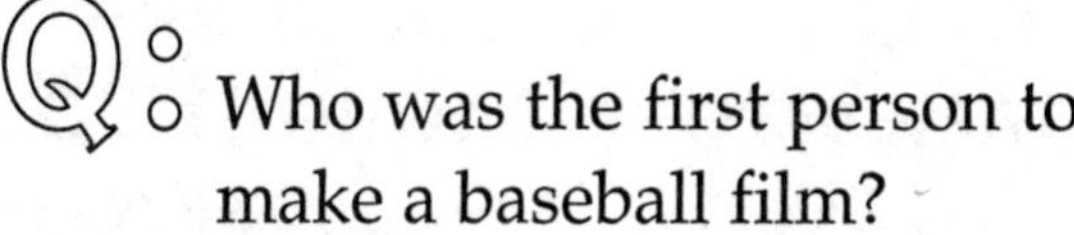

Q: Who was the first person to make a baseball film?

A: Thomas Edison

Extra Bases>

Edison created a single-reel work entitled *The Ball Game* in 1898.

MATCH UP BIZARRE OCCURRENCES AND THE GAMES THEY BROUGHT TO A PREMATURE CLOSE:

1. gnat swarm wrecks visibility
2. fans go wild on Disco Demolition Night
3. ten-cent beer night gets out of hand
4. fans pelt players with snowballs

A. Rangers vs. Indians, 1974

B. Cubs vs. Dodgers, 1946

C. White Sox vs. Tigers, 1979

D. Giants vs. Phillies, 1907

Answers: 1-B, 2-C, 3-A, 4-D

On July 17, 1914, at the moment Red Murray ran down a fly ball to seal a Giants victory in a twenty-one-inning contest against the Pirates:

A. America's entry into World War I was announced over the PA system.

B. A solar eclipse darkened the sky at the Polo Grounds.

C. A crazed fan shot the center fielder dead.

D. A disabled airplane landed in the Polo Grounds outfield.

E. A bolt of lightning struck the outfielder and knocked him unconscious.

Answer: E

True or False:

Unlike football, with the USFL and WFL, no rival league has tried to challenge the primacy of the American and National League during the twentieth century.

Answer: False

Extra Bases>

The Federal League took a crack at it in 1914–15, and featured teams such as the Brooklyn Tip-Tops, Chicago Whales, Kansas City Packers, and Newark Peppers.

NEWSPAPER COLUMNISTS PETE HAMILL AND JACK NEWFIELD ONCE NAMED THE THREE MOST EVIL MEN OF THE TWENTIETH CENTURY AS HITLER, STALIN, AND ______ .

Answer: Walter O'Malley

Extra Bases>

O'Malley was the Brooklyn Dodgers owner, who uprooted the team from Ebbets Field following the 1957 season and packed them off to L.A.

Q: Who was the first black player in the major leagues?

A: Fleet Walker

Extra Bases> Yes, Jackie Robinson broke the "color barrier" in 1947, opening up major-league baseball to blacks. But in baseball's infancy, before the "color barrier" had been more strictly codified, there was one—and only one—black player. Fleet Walker was a catcher for the Toledo Blue Stockings in the American Association. He played for just one season, 1884, and it must have been a trying one to judge from the comments of teammates such as pitcher Tony Mullane, who said Walker "was the best catcher I ever worked with, but I disliked a Negro and whenever I had to pitch to him I used to pitch anything I wanted without looking at his signals."

Who was not a member of the "$100,000 Infield," assembled by A's manager Connie Mack in the early 1900s?

A. Eddie Collins
B. Frank "Home Run" Baker
C. Jack Barry
D. Joe Dugan
E. Stuffy McInnis

Answer: D

Extra Bases>

Dugan was the A's shortstop in a later era; he joined the team in 1917.

TRUE OR FALSE:

The Yankees were the first team to wear pinstripes.

Answer: False

Extra Bases>

The Giants and Phillies introduced them during the 1911 season. The Yankees followed suit four years later.

COMMISSIONER FORD FRICKE ORDERED THAT AN ASTERISK BE OFFICIALLY PLACED BESIDE ROGER MARIS'S HOMER RECORD, DENOTING THE FACT THAT HE'D HIT 61 HOMERS DURING A ______-GAME SEASON, WHILE RUTH HIT 60 IN A ______-GAME SEASON.

Answer: 163, 155

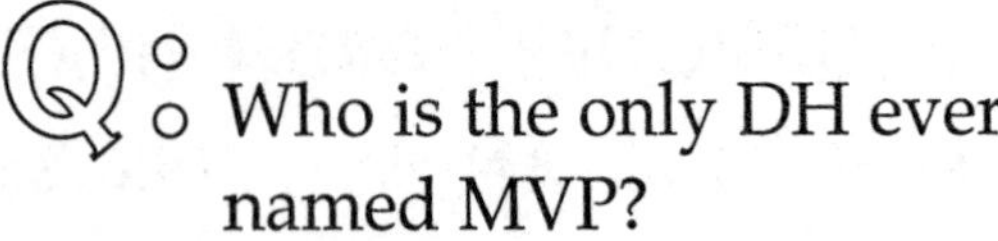

Q: Who is the only DH ever named MVP?

A: Don Baylor

Extra Bases>

He received the honor for his awesome 1979 season, in which he batted .296 with 36 HRs and 139 RBIs. He also scored a league-leading 120 runs that season.

WHICH TEAM HAD BASEBALL'S ONLY ALL-.400 OUTFIELD?

A. 1903 Pirates
B. 1913 A's
C. 1979 Expos
D. 1894 Phillies
E. 1927 Yankees

Answer: D

Extra Bases>

"Sliding" Billy Hamilton, in center field, batted .404. He was sandwiched on either side by "Big Sam" Thompson and "Big Ed" Delahanty, both of whom batted .407.

TRUE OR FALSE:

George Burns was the 1926 American League MVP.

Answer: True

Extra Bases>

But this was George Burns the Indians first baseman, no relation whatsoever to the late actor. He hit .358 with a league-leading 64 doubles and 114 RBIs.

MATCH PITCHERS WITH THEIR BREAD-AND-BUTTER PITCHES:

1. Charlie Hough	A. fastball
2. Tommy John	B. curveball
3. Bert Blyleven	C. knuckleball
4. Jim Maloney	D. sinkerball

Answers: 1-C, 2-D, 3-B, 4-A

In the case of Hall of Fame Pirate slugger Willie Stargell, "Willie" is short for ______.

Answer: Wilver

TRUE OR FALSE:

A team has fielded identical twins as a double-play combo.

Answer: True

Extra Bases>

Johnny O'Brien played second, brother Eddie took shortstop, for the Pirates in 1953. Topps put them on the same baseball card.

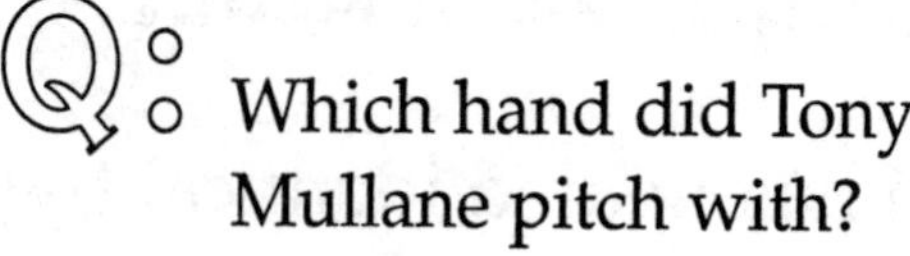

Q: Which hand did Tony Mullane pitch with?

A: both

Extra Bases>

Mullane was an ambidextrous journeyman pitcher who put together a 285–215 record between 1881 and 1894.

MATCH PLAYERS WITH THE CAUSES OF THEIR UNTIMELY DEATHS:

1. Lyman Bostock
2. Tim Crews and Steve Olin
3. Bo Diaz
4. Thurman Munson

A. boating accident
B. plane crash
C. gunshot
D. crushed by TV satellite dish

Answers: 1-C, 2-A, 3-D, 4-B

TRUE OR FALSE:

During the Cold War, the Russians claimed that the Americans stole base-ball from them.

Answer: True

Extra Bases>

They claimed baseball was merely a rip-off of their game "lapka."

WHO HAD THE HIGHEST SINGLE-SEASON BATTING AVERAGE IN BASEBALL HISTORY?

A. George Sisler
B. Nap Lajoie
C. Rogers Hornsby
D. Hugh Duffy
E. Tip O'Neill

Answer: D

Extra Bases> Duffy batted .440 for the NL Boston Beaneaters in 1894. But any of the others above would have been a good guess: George Sisler batted .420 for the Browns in 1922; Hornsby hit .424 in his best year with the Cardinals, 1924; Lajoie batted .426 for the Philadelphia A's in 1901; and Tip O'Neill batted .435 in 1887 for the St. Louis Browns of the American Association.

This book was typeset in Copperplate Gothic, Futura, and Palatino by Liane Fuji and Christine Weathersbee.

Calligraphy by Judith Stagnitto Abbate

Interior design by Nina Gaskin